Suburban Transformations

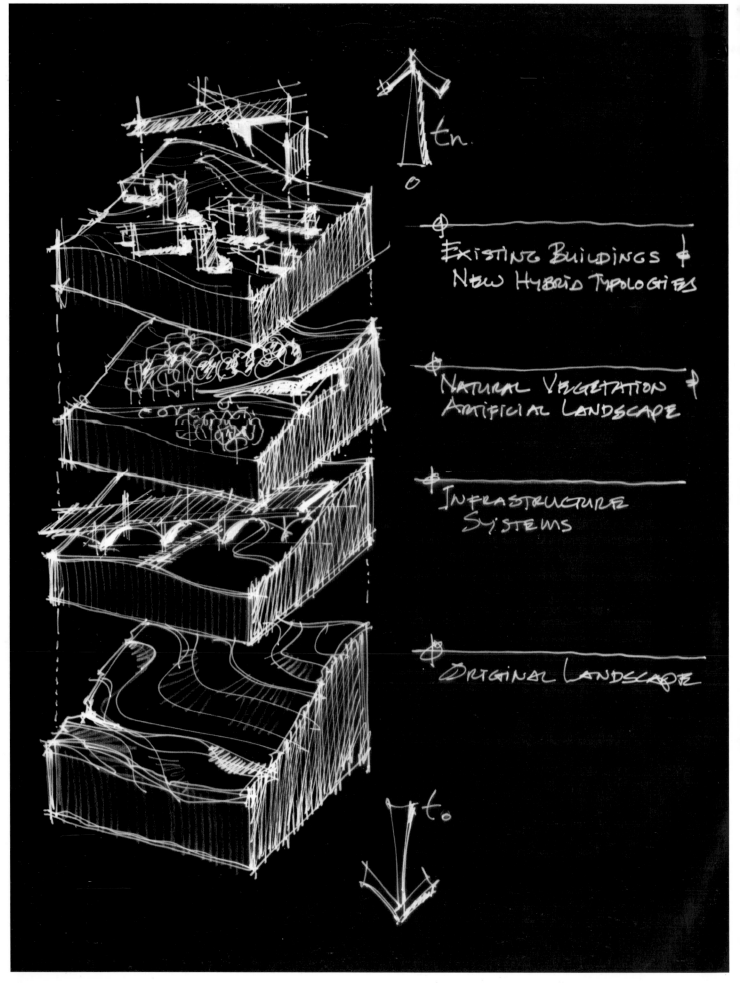

t_n

0

EXISTING BUILDINGS &
NEW HYBRID TYPOLOGIES

NATURAL VEGETATION
ARTIFICIAL LANDSCAPE

INFRASTRUCTURE
SYSTEMS

ORIGINAL LANDSCAPE

t_0

Suburban Transformations

Paul Lukez

Princeton Architectural Press
New York

Published by
Princeton Architectural Press
37 East Seventh Street
New York, New York 10003

For a free catalog of books, call 1.800.722.6657.
Visit our web site at www.papress.com.

Editor: Lauren Nelson Packard
Designer: Jan Haux

Special thanks to: Nettie Aljian, Sara Bader, Dorothy Ball, Nicola Bednarek,
Janet Behning, Becca Casbon, Penny (Yuen Pik) Chu, Russell Fernandez,
Pete Fitzpatrick, Wendy Fuller, Clare Jacobson, John King, Nancy Eklund
Later, Linda Lee, Katharine Myers, Jennifer Thompson, Arnoud Verhaeghe,
Paul Wagner, Joseph Weston, and Deb Wood of Princeton Architectural
Press —Kevin C. Lippert, publisher

Library of Congress Cataloging-in-Publication Data
Lukez, Paul, 1958-
Suburban transformations / Paul Lukez.
p.   cm.
Includes index.
ISBN 978-1-56898-683-8 (alk. paper)
1. Suburbs. 2. City planning. 3. Architecture—Social aspects.
4. Community life. I. Title.
HT351.L85 2007
307.74—dc22
                              2007018890

Contents

Preface

"Will we ever drag our visiting relatives out to show off our Edge City, our shining city on the hill?"
Joel Garreau, *Edge City* [1]

In his seminal book *Edge City*, Joel Garreau states, "Edge City's problem is history. It has none." He follows by speculating on the development of Venice, spanning over a thousand years, from its earlier "chaotic" form into a highly refined and interwoven assemblage of urban spaces and forms. Buildings were continually built, torn down, rebuilt, and altered, while the city's open spaces were sculpted and refined in response to the evolving demands of a growing city and its populace. The result of this thousand-year design and construction process is a richly woven tapestry of urban form and space, recognized by urban design experts today as a marvel in city planning. Yet, while the successes of the current configuration of the city are well documented, the most valuable lessons may lie in understanding how Venice's sometimes messy transformation over time came to be.

Regarding our relatively contemporary settlements—suburbs, exurbs, edge cities, and edge nodes—are we perhaps looking at the very early stages of new types of communities, whose mature forms have yet to crystallize, through successive and selective acts of writing and erasing buildings and spaces? What are the processes and design principles that might allow these relatively recent early community forms to develop into dynamic and memorable environments?

Throughout my academic and professional career, I have been interested in the relationship between time and architecture. In particular, I've been interested in how structures and their urban fabric change over time to accommodate new programs. These patterns of transformation reveal the behavior of form in response to changing circumstances. My fascination with understanding the vagaries of time led to the study of infrastructure elements and large municipal structures, as they were more likely to withstand entropy and because their mass could serve as repositories of time's accretions. I discovered that these kinds of structures often mutated into unusual typological configurations that defied conventional classifications.

The "traces" of these structures found in maps of richly layered cities suggest that the particularity of place is deeply rooted to time and circumstance. In an irreversible equation, the identity of a place cannot be altered: Venice, its structure and environment, can be of no other place. This quality of unique identity is lacking in current suburban contexts. Garreau's summation of the lack of history inherent in the edge city does not mean to imply that these contemporary sites are merely too recent, but that the processes that have engendered them deny transformation. There is a pathology to the contemporary development process that negates both Time and Circumstance.

The Adaptive Design Process, described in the pages of this book, explicitly incorporates time and circumstance into the design process. By mapping and cross-mapping the rich variety of features that make up any site, such as environmental features, topography, street patterns, building profiles, and sights and smells, opportunities for identity can be determined in even the most generic places. Carrying these mappings from the past on to the present and into the future in a series of "filmstrips" shows how a site is transformed over time, creating the essence of *place*.

This is a book for anyone who cares about the quality of their physical environment—particularly suburban and edge city sites—and wishes to see it improved, whether on the scale of building, community, or region. This includes planners, designers, town officials, policymakers, developers, landowners, environmental activists, and all those individual and institutional members of a community that have a stake or interest in shaping its future.

The book provides the reader with evocative images of just some of the multitude of strategies through which these goals can be achieved over time. The power of seeing what is possible, so much richer than the current reality, is the first step in activating new models for transforming our communities. The images included in the book transcend the limitations of visionary drawings; they are rooted in a process that constantly updates and recalibrates the projected reality within the limits of contemporary constraints. Yet the images have the potential to become iconic, in that they temporally register the dreams and aspirations of a community at a particular time.

Five case studies demonstrate the Adaptive Design Process. The study of Burlington, Massachusetts, your typical edge city, with its regional mall, speculative office buildings, corporate headquarters, strip malls, housing developments, and parking lots, provides a fine-grained illustration of the Adaptive Design Process in action. Tools such as mapping and cross-mapping are explained in depth using this extended case study. The other four case studies show the application of these ideas in edge cities that in various ways, are less than typical: Revere Beach, Massachusetts; Dedham Mall, Massachusetts; Shenzhen, China; and Amsterdam, the Netherlands. Each of these places exhibits certain conditions that are common to edge cities, but also have special differences, which can help illustrate the power of the Adaptive Design Process. In every case, site conditions and history are carefully mapped and analyzed and help inform future proposed transformations.

This book contends that it is conceivable that edge cities (and their suburban environs) could, over time, evolve into more habitable, cohesive, efficient, and memorable places with unique identities and histories, distinguishable from other edge cities and suburbs.

1 Joel Garreau, *Edge City: Life on the New Frontier* (New York: Random House, Inc., 1991), 9.

Acknowledgments

This book is about how suburbs and edge cities can evolve over time. Through successive acts of *erasure* and *writing* generated by multiple parties, richly layered places can be created.

Similarly, this book has evolved over time, sometimes through more *erasure* than *writing*, but always with the participation and assistance of many people, including mentors, teachers, colleagues, students, staff, editors, friends, and family. As an analysis of some of the most satisfying and beautiful cities can reveal, authorship is shared by the many who have contributed over time in ways, large and small, in realizing a city's final form. So too, this book is the result of multi-layered contributions over time.

While most of the content of this book was produced over the last five years, the book's genesis finds its origins in Kurt Forster's (my former Professor) evocative and inspiring lectures on urban palimpsests. Further study led me to the research of Prof. John Habraken, Prof. Ranko Bon, and Prof. Jan Wampler on *time* and *change* in the design of the built environment. I am deeply appreciative to both John and Jan, who served as generous mentors throughout my academic and professional career. Jan, in particular, demonstrated the enriching potential of integrating teaching, research, and practice.

The book itself was produced in successive waves of writing, and design, often overlapping with my teaching and research at MIT's Department of Architecture. It was Prof. Stanford Anderson who, while serving as Department Chair, generously supported the research that helped to advance the book's development. In addition, I am grateful to Dean Adele Santos, Dean William Mitchell, and Chairman Yung Ho Chang for their continued support of this project through its completion. The collegial encouragement of Prof. John De Monchaux, Prof. William Porter, Prof. Bill Hubbard, Prof. Larry Vale, Prof. Dennis Frenchman, Prof. Shun Kanda, and Jim Batchelor helped immeasurably at important moments. Prof. David Friedman strategic guidance and sustaining friendship helped push me through critical challenges and obstacles.

Early outlines and texts were developed with the advice, and editorial assistance of Pamela Hartford. Pamela's steadfast commitment to this project helped shape the structure of the book and its central arguments. Pamela Siska of MIT provided further editorial help and Erin Carlon finalized the book proposal. James Nuzum entered the project with fortuitous and uncanny timing. His insightful revisions and considerable editorial skill helped clarify the final text.

The design work was organized around teams both at MIT and my practice. Design workshops at MIT generated many of the initial conceptual investigations. The special contributions of my graduate students—Ariel Fausto, Mark Jewell, Chris Mulvey, Steven Jackson, Michael Spinelo, Pamela Cambell, Xin Tian, Otto Choi, Pablo Wenceslao, Marco Marranccinni, and Nicole Michel—helped to explore a wide array of theoretical and design issues. Mark and Xin's contributions in particular will always be cherished and valued.

Final design case studies were developed in my office (Paul Lukez Architecture) with the assistance of a multi-talented staff. The key contributors in the Burlington case study included Jason Hart, Pearl Tang, Heike Braungardt, Molly Forr, Chris Starkey, Sam Batchelor, Jian Zheng, Jue Zhan, Klemens Holzenbein, and Paul Lipchak. The Dedham e-Mall was developed primarily with the assistance of Matt Ostrow, whose design and computational skills astound. The Shenzhen proposal was coordinated by Tian Hao whose graduate research served as the foundation for the proposal's thesis. The design for the Amsterdam case study was based on the initial design developed by David Foxe, a graduate student who participated in Amsterdam design studio in 2005. The Amsterdam proposal was further developed by Derek Little, and Jian Xiang Huang at my office. The Revere project was generated for our visionary client, Joe DiGangi of Eurovest, and in close collaboration with George Tremblay, a partner at Arrowstreet Inc. Our urban design team was lead by Michael Gibson, working closely with Al Wei, and Jian Xiang Huang. Michael also led an inter-disciplinary research team comprised of eight MIT and Harvard graduate students.

Special thanks are extended to two designers, Ben Gramann and Jie Zhao, whose extraordinary design facilities touched most of the important design work and representations featured in the book. Ben and Jie worked closely with me over the past five years on many of the renderings and drawings.

The challenging task of formatting and compiling the over 1,000 images generated through multiple design phases was coordinated by Noura Alkhayat and

Foreword

Leslie Lok. With so many images, special attention was directed toward the graphic design of the images, diagrams and tables. Heart felt thanks are extended to Rachel Schauer, Matt Ostrow, Garrick Jones, and especially Sophie Kelle who found elegant solutions to graphically illustrating the Adaptive Design Process and other important diagrams.

I feel very fortunate to have been associated with our publisher, Princeton Architectural Press, and its outstanding editorial team. I am especially indebted to Clare Jacobson, the acquisitions editor, for supporting my proposal. Lauren Nelson Packard, the book's editor, has been a delight to work with throughout the editorial and production process. Her intelligent critique of the book and enthusiasm for the topic was always appreciated. Jan Haux deftly met the challenge of designing a book with over 300 images, carefully coordinated with text in a dynamic yet clear format. Lauren and Jan's shared vision, and their collective efforts were a model for collaboration.

And finally, I am forever beholden to my loving wife for her unwavering support of this book, despite the significant investment of time and resources required to complete it. The joyful rewards of watching my children (Alexander and Stephanie) mature sustained me over these past five years, as did their love and laughter. It is to my family that I dedicate this book with the deep gratitude and love of one who feels blessed beyond belief.

For the last half-century, Americans have spread themselves thinly across the landscape. But today the soaring cost, in financial and environmental terms, of inhabiting and navigating the suburbs has irrevocably changed the framework for analyzing the post-war settlement pattern. Budgets strain to the breaking point keeping the gasoline tank full for long commutes, and heating and cooling large detached homes. A tumultuous future awaits the planet if we continue to drive, waste energy, and pour emissions into the atmosphere.

Energy and climate change have become the new rationale for more compact, mixed-use, walkable and transit-oriented settlements, whether in new development or in existing cities. But few believe that will be enough. In addition to a new paradigm for future growth, we are also left with the dilemma of what to do with the built environment we've got—the vast exurban frontier, the extra-wide arterials serving big-box conglomerations and office parks, the single-family subdivisions built so enthusiastically by the corporate builders over acres of ranchland, farm fields, desert, and scrub forests, from Florida to the Central Valley.

How can these environments be retrofitted? Can they at all? That is the singular challenge for Paul Lukez in this book: to make more habitable cohesive places, with their own identity and unique quality of life, out of stretches of landscape created with very little design intention at all. A timelier guide to this invaluable exercise is hard to imagine. The field needs more analysis because, above all, it is staggeringly hard work. Not only is there no blank canvas, there is composition that must be radically altered, if not undone. The Lincoln Institute of Land Policy holds a seminar that describes this challenge similarly: Redesigning the Edgeless City.

Less alluring than the architectural wonder, more complex than any sketched New Urbanist village, the process of transforming the suburbs will, in the years ahead, become the highest calling for urban design. In these pages, practitioners will find an intriguing and innovative approach that promises to endure for many years to come.

Anthony Flint
Lincoln Institute of Land Policy
Cambridge, Massachusetts

The Development of Identity

As an old man looking across Lake Zurich in Bollingen, Swiss psychologist Carl Jung could see his life represented in the shapes and forms of his house. The house, consisting of towers, courtyards and walls, was started by Jung in 1926, and added to over time as his needs changed.[1] Jung's house is visually and temporally collapsed as a singular composition, such that causal relationships between the circumstances of his life and the forms they generated can be dissected. His beloved home became a repository of the memories of his life, his family and friends. It had an identity uniquely associated with a person, his unconscious, and a particular place in the world. Its form could be no different, as each decision was shaped in response to past decisions, existing conditions, and newly arising needs within the limits of available resources and materials. Like the fully formed identity of this man, the identity of the house was inextricably linked to a place, a community, and a landscape. A product of time and circumstance, its history is irreversible, its identity clearly and uniquely defined.

1 Dwelling Tower, 1923. C.G. *Jung, Memories, Dreams, Reflections* (New York: Vintage Books, 1989).

2 Bollingen, the final building, 1955. C.G. *Jung, Memories, Dreams, Reflections* (New York: Vintage Books, 1989).

As a society we can imbue our environments with the same richness of character and place so evident in Jung's house.[2] Our built environments can become repositories for the personal and collective memories of our lives as individuals and as members of communities. There are ways of layering and registering new social, economic, and cultural impetuses relative to natural and historic *traces*, allowing past, present, and the promise of the future to be suspended in temporal flux.

The creation of identity (as individuals and as a society) is central to our ability to orient ourselves in the world. Norwegian author and architect Christian Norberg-Schulz states that "today, we start to realize that true freedom presupposes belonging, and that 'dwelling' means belonging to a concrete place."[3] Jung's house became a concrete place of dwelling, one that allowed him the freedom to orient himself in the world, as the home itself was evolving.

Our evolving environments help us to orient ourselves as individuals and as a society. Every city or settlement pattern serves a purpose, whether it provides shelter, security, or economic, political, or social needs. The utility of a city is met in part through the design of the city's form, its systems, and their ability to support the activities required to sustain it. If the form does not match the intended use, then it will fail, and vice versa. Urban history is replete with examples of cities whose original uses and forms no longer met their respective requirements and capacity as they developed. This is especially true of cities caught in the upheavals of revolutionary or catastrophic change: natural, political, or economic. The ancient urban ruins of Mayan, Roman, Greek and other cultures illustrate how a city's original reason for being was no longer required, or how the services required to sustain a city could no longer be met by the form of the city and its supporting systems. Some structures fell and others rose in their place, creating a mix of old and new.

Traditionally, urban form has evolved over time, in cycles that were as much generational as epochal. The intended uses of early urban settlement patterns centered on providing shelter, protection, and access to shared resources and services. It was over time that each settlement sought to find the proper form that fit its use. Since resources and labor were limited, special care was taken to optimize the search for the proper fit between form and use. Determining the fit could very much be a function of the utilitarian as well as loftier cultural or aesthetic goals. The development of the gothic cathedral, for instance, represents the long and arduous task of finding the right match between cultural, religious, and spatial objectives within the material and engineering limits of stone and glass. The beauty that emerged out of this multi-century process is one that is dependant on the interaction and creative contributions of a multitude of craftsmen, artisans, and masons, from church to church, and generation to generation. And so it is with the development of urban form. The inhabited ruins of a Roman amphitheatre in the city of Florence, for instance, provides the perfect example of how a city can transform over time, how form follows fit over time. These spaces result from extended experiments in adaptations of form and space responding to dynamic economic and cultural forces.

Mapping the plan of the city makes clear that which is not at all obvious at street level. The original Roman amphitheater has through its traces left its mark on the city. Its oval shaped perimeter marks its old location, where houses and other buildings have enveloped it over time. As Roman culture faded and was replaced by subsequent regimes, its important civic interior space was filled in, sliced, and reconfigured in unusual and sometimes unexpected ways. Inhabitants transformed the carcass of the old amphitheater in ways that fit their immediate needs and values. Today, the site of the old amphitheater reflects the rich interplay of multiple parties engaging an urban environment over time to create an entirely new kind of urban configuration, defying easy typological categorization.

3 Plan of the Santa Croce district, Florence. Aldo Rossi, *The Architecture of the City* (Cambridge, Mass.: MIT Press, 1982).

The luxury of time allows for a longer, more finely tuned search for the proper fit, a luxury presumably not available in our age of hyper-accelerated development in the twenty-first century.[4] The dilemma we face is twofold: it centers on the speed and scale. Both factors add to the complexity of the task. Nevertheless, we are well positioned, if we so choose, to engage in the search for the right "fit" between the form and use of our suburban communities by working with the existing interventions and their residue, before erasing all traces of past interventions. Not only will we save resources, natural and man-made, but our energies will be focused on creating new and unexpected hybrid inventions.

Cologne: How a City Changes over Time

Cologne is a classic example of how a European city of Roman origin was transformed into a medieval walled city. As the medieval city continued to grow, its protective walls bulged and expanded, until a new ring of walls was required to support its ever-increasing population. As massive defenses and fortifications became obsolete in the nineteenth century, the walls and their expansive glaciers (large open fields separating the city walls from surrounding developments or encroachments) were no longer required. Consequently, valuable real estate was reclaimed through the demolition and destruction of the system of walls. Many cities have witnessed this kind of pattern, including Vienna, Munich, and Paris. But this phenomenon is about more than the walls and the spaces that bound growing communities. It is about how the underlying order of the original Roman city has been transformed over time. Traces of the original cardo and decumanus (the major north-south and east-west axes typical of Roman town planning) are still visible on contemporary maps. The lines of these axes may jog and shift from their original laser straight paths. Similarly, the block structures of the Roman colonies were absorbed into the amorphous sets of shapes and geometries that govern medieval city form. Cologne's form has been further enriched with complexity because, like Berlin, tumultuous historic forces, like the destruction of war, punctuate its history.

A Brief History

The Romans recognized the value of Cologne's location at the crossroads between east and west trade routes, and its strategic location along the Rhine River. The Roman governor Marcus Vipsanius Agrippa founded the city in 53 B.C. and built the city with the assistance of the local Teutonic tribe of Ubier. Together they built a city enclosed by 4.5 kilometers of walls, with twenty-one towers and nine gates. The city made good use of its location on the river and the island that ran parallel to its banks. Accessible by land and water, the island served primarily as a commercial/market area. Despite strong defenses, as an outpost of the Roman Empire, it came under continuous attack by the Franks, who overran the city in 260 AD. The last Roman governor left in 425 A.D.

The cultural dormancy of the Dark Ages left its mark on Cologne's development. The first expansions to the original Roman walls occurred in 950 A.D., when the commercial district of the island was enveloped in the new walls. In 1106 the largely rectilinear perimeter of the city walls began to "bulge" out in three locations, such that the shape of the city's new perimeter was more circular than square. By 1180, a new city wall, of greater girth, wrapped the expanding city. The area within the city included newly built churches as well as small farms and gardens. The city continued to flourish as a pilgrimage site, as the Relics of Epiphany were transferred to Cologne from Milan. The Cologne Cathedral's foundation was laid in 1248, and the city's coffers filled as it benefited from trade on the Rhine.

Pilgrimages decreased, however, and the city suffered an economic downturn. As a result, construction on the church stopped in 1560 and would not resume for another 282 years. In 1794, the French occupied Cologne and secularized this most Catholic city. Services were greatly improved, and immigration of Protestants and Jews was once again allowed. Combined with the emerging Industrial Revolution, Cologne built new rail links and bridges, establishing itself as a regional center of commerce. In 1880, the fourth wave of urban development further encircled the city in a "green belt." The former city walls were demolished and replaced with elegant tree-lined avenues serving new neighborhoods.

World War II brought massive destruction to the city and its monuments. Reconstruction has been extensive, and the suburbs have continued to grow beyond Fritz Schumacher's "green belt" in a radial pattern of development. Today, as Germany's fourth largest city, Cologne's form, despite the bombings, is rooted in its genesis as a Roman city and its subsequent transformation. The medieval marketplace, cathedral spires, and bridge spanning the Rhine serve as landmarks that orient residents and visitors alike and are emblematic of the city's rich past. The developed glaciers surrounding the city link together old and new. Cologne's robust economy, compact scale, gardens, surrounding landscape, and medieval core make it a dynamic and livable city.

4
Cologne, 900 A.D.
53 B.C.: Built and occupied as a Roman city. A 4.5 km-long city wall, with twenty-one towers and nine gates, circumscribes its center.
460: Cologne is conquered by the Franks.
881: The city is devastated by the Normans.

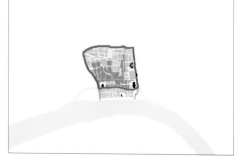

5
Cologne, 950 A.D.
950: Commercial quarter is enclosed by city walls.

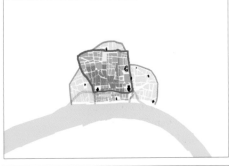

6
Cologne, 1106 A.D.
1106: City "bulges" outside
original city walls.

7
Cologne, 1180 A.D.
1180: City perimeter extended in
semi-circular pattern.

8
Cologne, 1880
1794: French occupy Cologne.
1822: Pontoon bridge built over
the Rhine.
1830: Rail lines established.
1859: Railway bridge built.
1873–1881: Expansion of city is
granted and completed.

9
Cologne, 1979
1881: Medieval wall is demolished.
1914: Right bank sector added
to city.
1917–1933: Fritz Schumacher's
green belt project extends
the city in a fourth ring.
1945: World War II leaves over
75 percent of Cologne in ruins.

Suburbia: A Study in Uniform Identity

On a purely aesthetic and cultural level, many critics have not been kind in their evaluation of suburbanization and its effects on the environment. Much quoted, James Howard Kunstler in *The Geography of Nowhere*, states that "eighty percent of everything ever built in America has been built in the last fifty years, and most of it is depressing, brutal, ugly, unhealthy, and spiritually degrading."[5] Kunstler goes on to suggest that the quality of "nowhereness" pervades the urban American landscape, and is the result of many factors, including the emphasis on designing objects in the landscape rather than the spaces between them, the focus on mobility, which by definition cannot be rooted to a place, and a banal housing stock. Douglas Kelbaugh, in *Common Place*, claims that the most evident architectural losses include a lack of architectural detail, human scale, authenticity, and varied building typologies.[6]

If the suburbs lack identity, some of it can be attributed to the commodification of architectural typologies associated with corporate entities (fast food, retailers, etc.) and their ubiquitous distribution across the country, making places more alike in order to market a consistent brand identity.[7] Home, and even community, has been turned into a commodity as well, less linked to a physical place than ever before.[8] Community is less about the relationships fostered and developed in a particular place than it is an image developed by corporations (as in the case of Disney's development of Celebration, Florida), bought or sold like a stock. The social and psychological link to place is secondary.

But commodification doesn't tell the whole story. The process of development and construction also contributes to the suburbs' lack of distinguishable identity. Suburbs resulted from a set of policies and bureaucratic controls unparalleled in American history.[9] Postwar housing construction was also a process that resulted in massive demographic shifts, urban to suburban, in a relatively short time period. Question arises as to whether an environment constructed in such haste can serve as an appropriate collective memory representing the work of a civilization.[10]

Landmarks allow us as individuals and a society to gauge our bearings both in space and in time, and to orient ourselves relative to the bearings of these markings. Churches, courthouses, rivers, streams, and monuments allow us to develop strong associations with places and feel secure in our identification with our place in the world. They are repositories for collective memory. Landmarks, physical and historic, are often absent in the suburbs because development has wiped away most traces of the past.

Suburbs are consuming storied landscapes at an alarming rate.[11] The amount of space and services generated in the suburbs per unit of infrastructure development is inefficient when compared to more compact urban settlement patterns.[12] This phenomenon is apparent when comparing the unmitigated growth of metropolitan areas such as Seattle, Washington, where the rate of land use outpaces population growth by more than a factor of two, to metropolitan areas such as Portland, Oregon. The city of Portland enforces limitations on development within an urban growth boundary that circumscribes the city's metropolitan area, acting as a contemporary variation on the medieval city wall, separating city from landscape.[13]

Sprawl is also eating up our wallets. Automobiles and the services and systems required to support their use cost on average about $6,000 per vehicle per year, and this is in 1997 dollars with 1997 fuel prices![14] Not all of these costs are apparent to drivers. Hidden subsidies for highway construction, maintenance, and defense spending required to maintain oil supplies limit the ability of consumers to analyze the true cost of their transportation decisions. Hidden also are the costs of infrastructure (e.g., sewer development, construction of schools, etc.), which are rarely considered when speculative housing developers apply for permits.[15]

On the macro scale, six of the ten largest corporations in the United States are in automobile and oil-related industries, contributing to nearly 20 percent of the American economy.[16] As foreign car manufacturers continue to carve out bigger segments of this economic sector, the stability of one of the pillars of the American economy is potentially endangered. In addition, the exclusive reliance on combustion-driven automobiles depletes a limited nonrenewable natural resource: oil. Discarding old automobiles and their hazardous waste endangers the environment by creating toxic landfills and polluting our ground water. Despite decades of scientific evidence highlighting the danger to the earth's air quality and depletion of the ozone, global warming remains a clear and present danger to our survival as a species.[17] The problem will become only more acute, as the use of automobiles escalates in an increasingly globalized world where all of its citizens seek to indulge in the liberating lifestyle offered by the individually owned and operated car.

Alternatives to Suburban Design: New Urbanism

Theoreticians, social scientists, planners, activists, urban designers, and architects have all sought to remedy suburbia's ills. The Congress for New Urbanism (CNU) founded by Peter Calthorpe, Andres Duany, Elizabeth Plater-Zyberk, Daniel Solomon, Liz Moule, and Stef Polyzoides in 1994 has dominated the debate on the suburbs. Their domination has been achieved in part through the prolific production of books, conferences, and built experiments. Effectiveness as a group goes beyond excellent organization. The ability to project compelling imagery of better places allows the CNU to neatly package its ideas to the larger public in a way that is both tangible and iconic.[18]

The movement's core values and principles are explicitly stated in its charter. It calls for a balanced investment in the cities and their suburbs, and for the protection of the outlying landscape. New Urbanists advocate integrating metropolitan and regional planning, as well as strengthening communities and neighborhoods. The charter recognizes that "design" on its own is not a panacea, and that social, economic, and policy issues are closely linked to resolving the problems associated with our suburban communities.[19] One of the group's central tenets is the importance of re-establishing a hierarchy of neighborhoods, their blocks, streets, and pedestrian networks, supported by public transit and connected to other neighborhoods and urban centers. The charter details more specific recommendations based on three levels: the metropolis, the neighborhood, and the block.

The husband and wife team of Andres Duany and Elizabeth Plater-Zyberk (DPZ) leads the so-called "East Coast" faction of the CNU, where the emphasis is on creating new suburban communities based on the principles of traditional neighborhood developments, developed in the late nineteenth and early twentieth century.[20] Some of these traditional communities, such as Radburn, New Jersey; Mariemont, Ohio; and Lake Forest, Illinois, were experimental "garden cities" inspired in part by the writings and designs of Ebenezer Howard, Patrick Geddes, and Fredrick Law Olmstead. These neighborhoods have a defined community center, systems of paths and open spaces, and a well-defined fabric of housing types. Designed to engender a strong sense of community, they are conveniently connected to larger urban centers by train but still removed from urban ills.

Duany and Plater-Zyberk have advanced the traditional neighborhood model through the extensive distillation of design guidelines. These guidelines govern the design of all of a community's physical elements, from its street and block organization, to the detail of curb cuts at intersections. Their best known projects include Seaside Florida (featured in the movie *The Truman Show*) and Kentlands, Maryland. Their designs for these new towns project all the imagery of community, albeit one that is built in a very short time and with an architectural language of another period.

10 Plan of Seaside, Florida. Courtesy of Duany Plater-Zyberk & Company.

11 Kentlands, Maryland. Courtesy of Duany Plater-Zyberk & Company.

While the East Coast School of CNU focuses on a nostalgic architectural and urban design vocabulary, the West Coast School's emphasis is on larger infrastructure, transit, and regional issues and their role in creating ecologically sensitive and pedestrian-friendly environments. Less concerned about continuity of architectural styles and typologies, the strength of their approach lies in an attempt to build communities around institutions, businesses, and housing linked by a network of transit, roadways, and pedestrian networks. Several projects in California embody these characteristics, including the "Gold Line TOD" in Pasadena, California; River Place in Portland, Oregon; and False Creek, Vancouver, B.C.

West Coast New Urbanists (such as Peter Calthorpe) shy away from the more prescriptive and formally driven design guidelines popular in the East. As a result, their proposals and their formal origins are less definitive, reflecting instead an adherence to spatial, material, and dimensional guidelines. Consequently, this approach is open to a wide array of influences, including mainstream architectural aesthetics.

Over the past fifteen years many bold New Urbanist experiments have been built. They have done a great deal to promote the public's awareness of sprawl, its problems, and potential solutions. They have helped foster transit-oriented, pedestrian-friendly, mixed-use neighborhoods, thereby reducing (in theory) reliance on the automobile. Principles of traditional town planning have been revived, yielding a wealth of useful precedents and typologies. The New Urbanist emphasis on the importance of the community in relationship to larger regional and ecological concerns has helped counter damaging development trends. They have made the connection between a community's form and its zoning regulations. Their designs engage in time-honored urban conventions of neighborhood, block, and street. Because of their attractiveness in branding and marketing, however, New Urbanist projects are often predictable and less likely to incorporate local idiosyncrasies and individual expression. Design solutions do not readily engage vibrant and contemporary architectural language and rely more on historical precedents—raising important cultural questions about our identity as a modern and evolving society. Further experimentation is needed to generate new identities that are unique to site and evolve over time. As currently formulated, New Urbanism alone cannot repair our suburbs and edge cities.

The Search for a New Synthesis, the Search for Fit

The Adaptive Design Process represents a new synthesis of a wide array of ideas, themes, and principles developed by architects, planners, and theoreticians concerned with urban and suburban form. It is intended to provide a comprehensive means for reforming edge cities and suburbs into unique places with their own distinct identities. The following principles guide and inform the Adaptive Design Process:

→ Evolving Identity over Applied Identity
→ Rooted to Place over Absent of Place
→ Historical over A-historical
→ Temporal over A-temporal
→ Acquired Meaning over Marketed Meaning
→ Community as Place over Community as Commodity

These themes are tightly interwoven and can be found in the works of the New Urbanists, radical Dutch urbanists, smart growth movement, new typologists, landscape architects, geographers, and urban morphologists that inform *Suburban Transformations*. All of these thinkers and designers concern themselves with the idea of *fit* in one way or another. Fit happens when urban form is uniquely matched to place or circumstance.

The search for the right fit between place and use can only happen over time. The impact of new interventions on existing contexts generates complex interactions between physical, ecological, social, and economic systems: interactions that go beyond our capacity to properly evaluate. Brasilia, for instance, presents the challenges of building instantaneous utopias. The oft-cited example of Levittown reveals a search for the proper fit between form and use, as inhabitants have altered the shapes and configurations of their homes and community to meet their needs. Both of these adaptations to form, to find its proper fit, happened by accident. Whereas the planned portion of Brasilia's design resulted from a "closed system" driven by government coordinated development processes, Levittown, after its initial monolithic and instantaneous development and construction process, engaged the open systems available in the marketplace to generate change. The challenge lies

in finding open and dynamic processes that can operate on all scales of development, regional to individual, such that societal forces can be harnessed and engaged over time for the productive improvement of our environment and the enhancement of our culture and its people. Mapping techniques that can record landscape features, highlight interrelations existing on a site, trace transformations over time, and provide for a mechanism to project transformations into the future are essential to the task of finding fit over time.

Mapping offers designers the ability to discover, record, and communicate complex site features and relationships. The study of urban morphology is well positioned to inform suburban design because it tracks the changing structure of urban tissue. It is a field that studies the historical process that generates form.[21]

The geographer M.R.G. Conzen, began mapping and analyzing the relationships between the streets, plots, and building typologies in Newcastle, Birmingham, and other English towns in the early twentieth century.[22] Conzen examined how each combination of forms was unique to the circumstances found on the site.[23] What he found was that parcels were critical to understanding the order of a town's evolution, as the definition of parcels is directly linked to power and control. Zoning, ownership, and other factors provide valuable insight into understanding the typologies present on a site and can also be useful for projecting future transformations. The role of plotting and parceling of land is especially relevant to suburban settings because, unlike the very regular and predictable patterns found in old English towns, they are characterized by unique and unpredictable parceling arrangements that reflect U.S. history and track legal and financial arrangements that are particular to each state, city, county, and town. Understanding these idiosyncrasies could lead to interesting design solutions for suburbs.

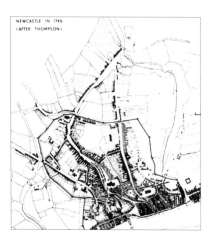  

12 Left: Newcastle in 1746 (after Thompson). Center: Newcastle in 1770 (after Hutton). Right: Newcastle in 1830 (Oliver's plan). © M.R.G. Conzen.

Urban morphologist James Vance built on Conzen's ideas by outlining the processes involved in morphogenesis, which includes land assignment, connection, initiation and transformation through adaptation.[24] Vance saw beyond a formal and physical analysis of the city's structure by taking into consideration capital accumulation and transfers, speculation, and market forces in his analysis, long considered a weakness of the Conzen School.[25] Vance's mapping techniques therefore give us a tool for understanding how, for example, a farm subdivided for tract housing might later on be recombined for large scale commercial development; it has to do with improving capital flows, or how much revenue a piece of land can produce.

Professor Emeritus of MIT John Habraken gives us yet another way of understanding urban form by mapping the various levels of control and decision making power on a site. For Habraken, the arcaded streets of Bologna, the ruins of Pompeii, Amsterdam's canal lined blocks, and Boston's Back Bay neighborhood, provide rich examples of urban tissue that has been inhabited and altered over time to meet the needs of its inhabitants.[26] These environments can be viewed through a filter of levels, representing different scales of control from block to street to building to room. Habraken's mapping techniques show how territorial control is exercised over a site and its structures by its inhabitants. In any suburb or edge city, territory is controlled in ways that reflect various levels of national, state, county, city, neighborhood, and individual interests. All of these influences are strong determinants of how land is inhabited and controlled.

13 Map of Pompeii illustrating an "urban tissue" comprised of a courtyard typology, transformed to meet the needs of different users over time. John Habraken, *Transformations of the Site* (Cambridge, Mass.: Awater Press, 1988).

The great landscape architect Ian McHarg provides a tool for understanding the interconnectedness of natural systems by overlaying or cross-mapping separate ecological systems that play a role on a site. In his seminal book *Design with Nature*, through case studies of communities on the outskirts of Washington, D.C. and Philadelphia, McHarg provides "an ecological manual for the good steward who aspires to art." For McHarg, this art involves bringing into balance the needs of the human environment with the natural environment, recognizing that "in order to endure we must maintain the bounty of the great cornucopia which is our inheritance."[27] His beautifully illustrated book lays out strategies and processes that distill information about the landscape and the needs of contemporary urban development through a "physiographic" mapping process. With great foresight and inventiveness that preceded the development of Geographical Information Systems (GIS),[28] McHarg laid one transparent map of information about the site's ecology and physical attributes over another, like a "complex X-ray photograph with dark and light tones."[29] Together, these composite maps reveal important values and opportunities for future designs, which consider the multitude of natural forces operating on a site. McHarg's mapping techniques inspired the cross-mapping techniques discussed later in this book. Instead of just overlaying the different ecological systems at work on a site the Adaptive Design Process examines all systems operating on a site, from environment to infrastructure, plots, and capital flows. Through graphically comparing relevant community features, interesting relationships that make up identity can be discovered and enhanced over time.

Building on the McHargian tradition, Anuradha Mathur and Dilip da Cunha have documented, through lush and rich visuals, the shifting landscape of the Mississippi River. Challenging the Army Corp of Engineers' vision of the river as an object that "arrest[s] time through hydrology," Mathur and da Cunha attempt to define the Mississippi "as a dynamic, living phenomenon that asserts its own dimensions."[30] It is the journey to understand this river that led to this extraordinary compilation of maps, charts, sections, paintings, phototransects, and silk-screens, highlighting the behavior and conflicts that arise in the relationship between a powerful natural system, like the Mississippi, and man's attempt to inhabit its boundaries.

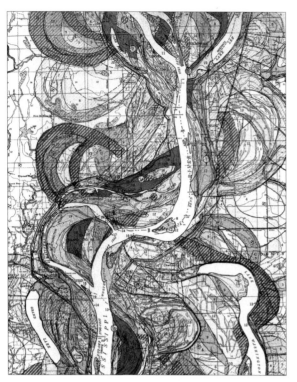

14 Harold Fisk's 1944 maps of the Mississippi River provide a beautiful example of how natural systems such as rivers can change over time.

typological inventions can fundamentally reconsider function and form, as well as building and landscape. The middle landscape, in Rowe's mind, is an area ripe for experimentation and discovery.[34]

Other designers have embraced typological invention as a means of reordering and repairing the suburban condition as well. Steven Holl, author of *Edge of a City*, envisions hybrid typologies and new programs that help mediate the edge between landscape and metropolis.[35] Moshe Safdie extrapolates typologies from contemporary mega-structures, which are endemic to suburbs, and turns them into multi-layered, intermodal urban centers.[36] Collectively, the strength of these proposals lies in their ability to inspire the invention of new forms of urbanity rooted to contemporary programs, sites, and conditions.

Mapping ultimately leads back to the search for typological fit. The search for fit between form and use can be developed over time, such that form follows use over time. As the use changes, the form must accommodate the new use, unless the performance parameters (spatial, material, and cultural) of a particular use are malleable. If this reciprocal relationship between form and use cannot find a temporally dynamic equilibrium, by definition, the form (the city and its buildings) will die; this is one reason for the decline of suburbs and edge cities. It also argues for the invention of new building typologies that can better serve and enhance our suburbs.

Many architects have devoted their careers to devising new kinds of buildings and form. They are not bound by a common ideology or organizational affiliations, yet their speculations on suburban pathology show great promise in defining forms and processes to reconcile place with the "space of flows."[31]

Peter Rowe terms the area between country and city the "middle landscape." He views the problem of constructing the middle landscape as one of reconciling the object in the field.[32] He proposes the use of poetic operations such as juxtaposition, scaling, and ordering to generate new building typologies.[33] Numerous examples of proposals generated by his Harvard GSD graduate students illustrate how edge city corridors have been transformed. Taken together, these projects suggest that

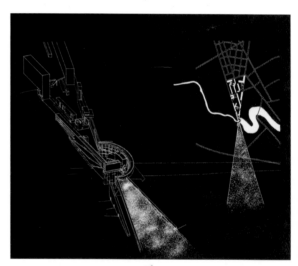

15 A hybrid dam structure for Cleveland that could support multiple public programs. Steven Holl, *Edge of a City* (New York: Princeton Architectural Press, 1991).

Radical Dutch urbanists have generated new typologies that mix infrastructure, landscape, and buildings. For example, Koolhaas's urban vision, expressed in Eurallile, a high-speed train station and multimodal urban center in Lille, France, shares the Futurists' view of Sant'Elia's studies for the Citta Nuova, a city built around its infrastructure and conceived of as movement, not stasis. The radical proposals for Lace, a new type of urban form conceived by the Dutch firm MVRDV, create new motorway configurations, such as a "roulade," that are "transmuted into a vertical bundle of roads" where quiet, energy-efficient cars weave at high speed past, and to, fluidly defined destinations.[37] The hyper-efficient system of laced roadways creates unusual opportunities for building alongside, over, and under this new network of places. Similar opportunities exist in American suburbs and edge cities where infrastructure and development are inextricably, though less than elegantly, linked. A mall, its parking lot and access roads for example are linked, but banally so.

Monolab, another Dutch offshoot of the Office for Metropolitan Architecture (OMA), has generated a multitude of proposals for the Dutch Ministry of Spatial Planning. Many of these proposals focus on the development of an infrascape, "a grid in which infrastructure—in this case freeway, beltway, conventional and high-speed railway tracks—is interwoven with city and landscape."[38] Infrascape projects have also created strategies for developing underutilized land between the boundaries of the motorway and its adjacent urban settlements, as well as over highway intersections to create colossal structures of land, form, and infrastructure.

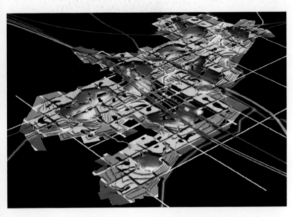

16 The Breda Sands infrascape supports infrastructure and a multitude of uses in and about a shell of artificial landscape. © Monolab Architects.

Hybrid typologies such as the infrascape could provide satisfying and efficient design solutions that are currently unknown to American suburbs where farm abuts subdivision, buses ply major roads that are unfriendly to pedestrians, and amenities and infrastructure cut up large tracts of otherwise intact landscapes.

The Smart Growth approach seeks to remedy the ever-outward march of development by redeveloping brownfields, empty lots, and concentrating new development among existing structures. Time is engaged through acts of "repair" and "infill," as the old and new coexist side by side in an ever-evolving community. By working within constrained boundaries, these processes can in turn generate new and sometimes unexpected spatial-temporal typologies that emerge out of necessity. Unique and idiosyncratic urban configurations with strongly rooted identities are created. Like the radical Dutch urbanists, smart growth advocates embrace infrastructure. Building along existing roads, sewer lines, power transmission lines, and other forms of infrastructure not only saves money, but also saves forests, farms, wetlands, and other landscapes from development.

William McDonough and Michael Braungart explore other ways to protect the environment that could involve new typologies and building methods. In their book *Cradle to Cradle* they stray from a restrictive view of environmental protection, characterized by the four R's (reduce, reuse, recycle, and regulate), and advocate for design that is based on lifecycles. Biological metabolism serves as a metaphor for processing waste such that waste becomes generative.[39] Buildings could produce their own power and convert their own waste into useful products such as clean water and vegetation. The city itself can be recycled according to lifecycles. Long lifecycle features such as infrastructure provide the backbone for development, while short-lived features such as retail outlets could be flexible and constantly reconfigured and reprogrammed.

Anne Vernez Moudon takes a morphological view of San Francisco's Alamo Square area and documents how this neighborhood has been able to accommodate the demographic shifts of a growing urban center. The adaptability and flexibility of this neighborhood can be attributed in part to the design of the city block structure as well as the buildings. A detailed analysis of the wood-framed building types reveals a highly "resilient" system of component assemblies, yielding multiple spatial and territorial definition that is never limited to a finite form of architectural expression.[40] Neighborhoods that are designed to accommodate change not only create more unique community identities, but also are more likely to survive societal and demographic shifts. Stuart Brand calls designed adaptability "scenario buffered building." The building is "treated as a strategy rather than a plan."[41]

The ravaged streets and buildings of war-torn Sarajevo serve as the canvas upon which Lebbeus Woods argues for a different kind of renewal. War levels cities and "reduces their multi-layered complexity of means to one-layered *tableaux*."[42] Woods makes a case against restoring or erasing the ruins of war-torn cities (as was the case in so many European cities—Frankfurt, Munster, etc.), and instead suggests building upon the existential remnants of war.[43] The city is renewed piecemeal, with recycled fuselages, military hardware, and building fragments. Through a process of urban injections, built relative to the city's scars and scabs, new spaces are created for public and private use. Out of the reconstituted remnants of war, a new tissue develops, reflecting the changing matrix of conditions.[44] Suburbs are laid waste not by warfare, but by economic forces and a natural cycle of decay. Over time and through a process of erasure and writing, suburbs can become unique places, imbued with their own distinctive identities.

Time is of the essence. Engaging time in design is what creates a strong sense of identity. In *The Architecture of the City,* Aldo Rossi illustrates how "Urban Artifacts" such as the Palazzo della Ragione in Padua, have evolved and developed over the centuries into complexly configured urban forms, housing markets, public halls, and services. Devastated by hurricanes in 1425, the Palazzo della Ragione's position in the urban fabric has evolved to fit the built environment, adjacent plazas, and their unique geometries. As part of the structure of the city, its individuality "depends on being a complicated entity which has developed in both space and time."[45] But Rossi's interest is not only in the urban artifacts that comprise a city, but the city itself as a "gigantic man-made object, a work of engineering and architecture that is large and complex and growing over time."[46] For Rossi, time is a historical process as well as a chronological process that can be measured against urban artifacts of different periods.[47] The American suburbs represent for him "amorphous zones" where the accelerated transformation processes "represent inconclusive times in the urban dynamic."[48] By inference, these amorphous zones lack the unique identities provided by urban artifacts such as the Palazzo della Ragione and their ability to impart knowledge about the "identity, locus, design and memory" of the city and its artifacts.

Time is not part of the equation that consciously generates the suburban context, yet the suburb is subject to the same forces of transformation processes as any built context, albeit at an accelerated rate. The active engagement of temporal factors in the design of suburban contexts, which is the purpose of the Adaptive Design Process, yields a more life-enhancing environment where the past and future are contained in the present. The search for new and unusual hybrid building typologies can create building and landscape configurations that are unique to a specific time and place. By virtue of their unique identity, these time markers serve to orient the public, spatially and historically. Set within an evolving urban tissue, flexible, adaptable, and resilient to the different cycles of change, the form of a community could follow its use, dynamically and reciprocally over time.

Endnotes

1   C.G. Jung, *Memories, Dreams, Reflections* (New York: Vintage Books, 1989).

2   For a discussion on the character of the landscape as an extension of a site's "personality," originating in Ancient Greece, see Norberg-Schulz, *Genius Loci: Towards a Phenomenology of Architecture* (New York: Rizzoli International Publications, 1980), 28.

3   Ibid., 22.

4   Compare the extended development cycles of a Venetian Plaza, with the near instantaneous development of post–World War II mass housing complexes, such as Bijlemeer (in the Netherlands) or Pruitt-Igoe (St. Louis, Missouri), designed to house thousands of families in uniform apartment blocks. The search for the fit never materialized and the communities have failed.

5   James Howard Kunstler, *The Geography of Nowhere* (New York: Simon & Schuster, 1996), 10.

6   Douglas Kelbaugh, *Common Place: Toward Neighborhood and Regional Design* (Seattle, Wash.: University of Washington Press, 1997), 40.

7   Ibid., 41. Identity is linked to the commodification of architectural typologies and style.

8   Alex Marshall, *How Cities Work: Suburbs, Sprawl, and the Roads Not Taken* (Austin, Tex.: University of Texas Press, 2000), xvi.

9   Richard Moe and Carter Willkie, *Changing Places: Rebuilding Community in the Age of Sprawl* (New York: Henry Holt and Company, 1997), 55.

10   Ibid., 260.

11   Between 1982 and 1992 the U.S. lost 400,000 acres of prime farmland every year to sprawl. Terry S. Szold and Armando Carbonell, *Smart Growth: Form and Consequences* (Toronto, Ontario, Canada: Webcom LTD., 2002), 169.

12   Robert Burchell and Anthony Downs, *Sprawl Costs: The Economic Impacts of Unchecked Development* (Island Press: Washington, D.C., 2005).

13   Portland's land use is projected to increase by 6 percent by 2040, while its population will grow by 77 percent. Kelbaugh, *Common Place*, 27.

14   Jane Holtz Kay, *Asphalt Nation: How the Automobile Took over America* (New York: Crown, 1997), 120.

15   "The true cost of sewer service alone to a new home ranges from $2,700–$25,000." This figure does not include the costs of road, utilities and schools, rarely offset by "impact fees." Kelbaugh, *Common Place*, 33. See also Robert Burchell and Anthony Downs, *Sprawl Costs: Economic Impacts of Unchecked Development* (Washington, D.C.: Island Press, 2005).

16   Kay, *Asphalt Nation*, 123.

17   The United States emits "nearly one fifth of the world's greenhouse gases

annually" despite comprising less then 5 percent of the world's population. See Kelbaugh, *Common Place*, 35.

18   The imagery is so compelling that Hollywood used one of its first experiments, Seaside, Florida, for the backdrop of the movie, *The Truman Show*.

19   Peter Calthorpe, *The Regional City* (Washington, D.C.: Island Press, 2001), 279–85.

20   See Andres Duany et al., *Suburban Nation: The Rise and Fall of Suburbia* (New York: North Point Press, 2000). Also see Andres Duany and Elizabeth Plater-Zyberk, *Towns and Town-Making Principles*, ed. Alex Krieger with William Lennertz (New York: Rizzoli, 1991).

21   Anne Vernez Moudon, "The Changing Morphology of Suburban Neighborhoods," in Petruccioli, *Typological Process and Design Theory* (Cambridge, Mass.: Aga Kahn Program for Islamic Architecture at Harvard University and Massachusetts Institute of Technology), 141.

22   J.W.R. Whitehand, *The Urban Landscape: Historical Development and Management* (New York: Academic Press, Inc., 1981), 1.

23   Ibid., 14.

24   James E. Vance Jr., *The Continuing City: Urban Morphology in Western Civilization* (Baltimore, Md.: Johns Hopkins University Press, 1990), 33–35.

25   Spiro Kostoff, *The City Shaped* (London: Bulfinch Press, 1991), 26.

26   John Habraken, *Transformations of the Site* (Cambridge, Mass.: Awater Press, 1988), 145.

27   Ian McHarg, *Design with Nature* (New York: John Wiley & Sons, 1992).

28   In the interest of limiting length, this text does not outline the numerous and exciting advances made in GIS and their potential as a transformation tool. See Brail and Kosterman, *Planning Support Systems* (ESRI Press); Leong and Koolhaas, eds. *Ulterior Spaces, Harvard Design School Guide to Shopping*. For a compilation of projects which incorporate GIS to document and analyze historic sites and events see: Knowles, *Past Time, Past Place*.

29   McHarg, *Design with Nature*, 39.

30   Anuradha Mathur and Dilip da Cunha, *Mississippi Floods: Designing a Shifting Landscape* (New Haven, Conn.: Yale University Press, 2001), xii.

31   Manuel Castells refers to "space of flows" (as a dispersed system of "information generating units" independent of topography, and history), which will replace the "space of places." See Manuel Castells, *The Informational City: Informational Technology, Economic Restructuring and the Urban-Regional Process* (Oxford: Basil Blackwell, 1989) 126.

32   Peter Rowe, *Making the Middle Landscape* (Cambridge, Mass.: MIT Press, 1991), 249.

33   Ibid., 276.

34   Ibid., 291.

35   Steven Holl, *Edge of a City* (New York: Princeton University Press, 1991), 9.

36   Moshe Safdie, *The City After the Automobile: An Architect's Vision* (New York: Basic Books, 1997), 139.

37   Winy Mass, *FARMAX* (Rotterdam, the Netherlands: 010 Publishers, 2006), 454.

38   Hans Ibelings et al.,*The Artificial Landscape: Contemporary Architecture, Urbanism, and Landscape Architecture in the Netherlands* (Rotterdam: NAI Publishers, 2000), 134. See also www.monolab.nl.

39   William McDonough and Michael Braungart, *Cradle to Cradle* (New York: North Point Press, 2002) 53.

40   Moudon describes "resilient" spaces which can be "reinterpreted and used in a variety of ways while keeping most of its original shape, dimensions, access, fenestration, finishes, and services. A resilient space should provide inhabitants with a great deal of control over what can be done with the space without undue modification." See Anne Vernez Moudon, *Built For Change: Neighborhood Architecture in San Francisco* (Cambridge, Mass.: MIT Press, 1986), 179.

41   Stewart Brand, *How Buildings Learn: What Happens After They Are Built* (New York: Viking, 1994), 178.

42   Lebbeus Woods, *Radical Reconstruction* (New York: Princeton Architectural Press, 1997), 8.

43   Ibid., 14.

44   Ibid., 36.

45   Aldo Rossi, *The Architecture of the City*: (Cambridge, Mass.: MIT Press, 1982), 29.

46   Ibid.

47   Ibid., 96.

48   Ibid., 95.

In Search of Identity over Time

Time-Layered Sites

Great cities of the world all evolved over time. Paris wasn't created in a single day, a single stroke, or a single master plan. Cities follow infrastructure, be it a river, canal, bay, plain, or road and then transform over time. There are many examples of rich time-layered cities, which serve as repositories for man's intervention with site. Such evolving sites show how individuals and institutions have sought to find the right fit between places and the societies they support. This process of searching for the form of a place creates opportunities for individuals and their institutions to "dwell" in their environments, thereby allowing individuals to orient themselves spatially and temporally relative to larger societal forces. What then are the factors that contribute to creating richly layered sites?

A number of factors create a sense of place including the landscape, people, building and infrastructure typologies, and cultural and aesthetic imperatives driving a society. While the qualities of a site, typologies, or cultural imperatives may vary from place to place, each shares a process of "erasing" and "writing" on the site. Some historical patterns of transformation include:

→ Overlaying cultural and aesthetic ideals on complex sites
→ Layering cities and societies over time
→ Superimposing infrastructure: infrastructure follows infrastructure
→ Bounded environments: natural, political, or other constraints
→ Cities claiming land from the sea
→ Hyper-development: fusing infrastructure and served spaces

These are but a few of the many types of possible transformation themes. Although the circumstances differ, the subtext that runs through these precedents is an emphasis on infrastructure as a physical system that binds site to city and the people it serves.

By reviewing actual transformation patterns we can begin to identify patterns of change; we also can speculate on how to project these transformation patterns onto contemporary suburban conditions, to generate richer time-layered environments.

Overlaying Cultural and Aesthetic Ideals on Complex Sites: Pergamon

Through a convergence of favorable historic circumstances (bountiful natural resources, peace, prosperity, technological and intellectual advancements), some societies have been able to shape their environments so that they go beyond basic utility. They seek the highest cultural and aesthetic objectives. One such environment is the Hellenistic city of Pergamon, located in Asia Minor. It is an example of how a minimal yet consistent set of building types (the stoa, the temple, and the theater) can be applied and adjusted to a topographically challenging site. This visually and aesthetically sophisticated ensemble of buildings was designed and built over hundreds of years. Each building relates to other buildings as well as local and remote landscape features. Often, a structure played a dual role. For instance, the Temple of Athena can be viewed within the constraints of a carefully choreographed visual sequence, set up by gates and embracing stoa-like forms that create its sanctuary. This same temple, however, can also be prominently viewed from the theater located below the temple plateau. The master builders of the Hellenistic era were able to develop a sensitively calibrated environment, one that recognized the limits of building technologies (stone column and lintel system) while still pursuing aesthetic ideals of the highest order.

1 Pergamon: Celebrating a sophisticated aesthetic ideal

Layering Cities and Societies over Time: From Rome to the Industrial Era

Europe offers numerous examples of how Roman settlements like Cologne evolved into vibrant medieval markets only to be transformed once again in the Industrial era. Roman military outposts were strategically located close to a river or other militarily critical position. Based on a cross-axial pattern, the military camps were laid out in similar ways, with predetermined locations for barracks, armories, and senior staff quarters. As the Roman Empire disintegrated, the rigidity of the street patterns and walls broke down over time through the in cremental process of erasure and writing. With the emergence of medieval city-states, and the corresponding need for them to serve as both open markets for townspeople and secure bastions, the remnants of the Roman settlements were continually transformed. City walls were reinforced or rebuilt to define the town, its market, and some fields. As a town's population expanded, its interior was filled in with additional houses, shops, and workshops. The competition between forces of commerce and habitat resulted in richly layered and organic street patterns, which create the pedestrian experience so greatly appreciated by tourists today.

Superimposing Infrastructure: Infrastructure follows Infrastructure

Perimeter City, outside of Atlanta, Georgia, is an example of how even relatively recent cities can evolve as one system of infrastructure is built alongside, on top of, over, or under previous networks. A web of Native American trails around Atlanta evolved into military roads connecting settlers' fortifications. As the region was secured and land was cleared for farming, accessible roads were needed to bring goods to market. More roads followed and were augmented by rail lines to and from local and regional centers. As regional centers (primarily Atlanta) increased, they needed more space for housing, commerce, and industry. Coupled with generous government subsidies in the 1950s and 1960s, massive highways were developed over the farms and their rail and road networks. Today, Perimeter City is an important node in Atlanta's polycentric metropolitan area. Traces of the earliest Indian paths, settlers' trails, and rail lines are still evident in the physical ordering of this community and its extensive retail, office, and housing complexes, and their relationship to greater Atlanta.

Bounded Environments: Natural, Political, or Other Constraints

Where a growing city encounters few, if any, natural, legal, social, or economic boundaries, it will grow in all directions without restraint, like milk spilled on a flat surface. If, however, there are natural, legal, or other constraints limiting growth, the development will be confined within a visible or virtual envelope. This phenomenon is evident in the satellite photographs taken of the San Francisco Bay Area over the last thirty years, which clearly show how the steep topography surrounding the bay has limited development to areas with minimal slopes. Portland, Oregon, on the other hand, has legally defined growth boundaries within which development is to be concentrated. In both cases, constraints result in efficient use of land and resources within the city. Residents, developers, builders, and designers have discovered innovative ways to maximize space within these limits. These environments become intensely layered with few left over and neglected spaces visible. Necessity generates invention, and consequently, cities like San Francisco and Portland have developed unique identities resulting from the overlapping domains of constraints and possibilities.

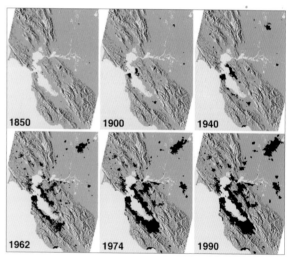

2 Urban growth in the San Francisco Bay Area

Cities Claiming Land from the Sea

Where land and sea come together to create ideal ports or centers of commerce, the expanding needs of a growing city can exceed the available land. Cities like Boston and Oakland drain waterways or fill existing wetlands to create new land for development. Over several hundred years, Amsterdam has claimed land from the "sea" or, more specifically, the Ij River and its surrounding wetlands. Dikes are built and shallow waters drained to provide additional land and capacity for serving local, regional, and international markets. Based on a unique pattern of concentrically layered blocks and canals, the city expanded outwardly canal-by-canal, block-by-block. Canals not only drain water from the soggy ground, they also help boats navigate directly from harbor to warehouse. To this day, Amsterdam is claiming land from the river Ij to meet the need for additional housing and recreational spaces. The challenge of meeting the needs of land-bound residents without suffocating the commercial needs of a harbor has generated unusual configurations of waterways and reclaimed land, unique and particular to this place.

3 Amsterdam

Hyper-development: Fusing Infrastructure and Served Spaces

In certain places (Manhattan and Hong Kong) where land is extremely limited and populations incredibly dense, hyper-development is the only alternative. Hyper-development is characterized by extremely high-density developments, where multiple uses occupy a site. Unusual building typologies (often combined with infrastructure) result and "left over" land or space is maximized. Often, as in the case of Hong Kong, the distinction between infrastructure and "served spaces" is ambiguous at best. The competition for space is so great that in order for the infrastructure to function, its physical configuration intrudes on private spaces and vice versa. Land below and above highways and bridges are utilized, as are slivers of space sandwiched between buildings and infrastructure. In Tokyo, for instance, landscape and parks are sometimes redefined as a form of infrastructure, where housing is built over, alongside, and within the more traditional boundaries of a park's protected spatial precinct. Even at the turn of the nineteenth century, the space below Otto Wagner's elevated rail lines in Vienna were inhabited by workshops. Rome is full of examples where the ruins of aqueducts have been parasitically inhabited by legions of citizens seeking shelter. Similarly, a recent highway extension project in Seoul, Korea cuts right through an existing housing block. The block was structurally reinforced, but not removed, despite increased noise and pollution. Hyper-development challenges our definitions of public and private spaces.

The transformations that have defined places as old as Pergamon or as new as modern day Tokyo, can be looked at in their simplest form: as a series of operations or steps that add or take away material from a site. Identity arises out of an accumulation of these steps and can be represented as an equation.

IDENTITY = SITE + TIME

Examples of time-layered sites reveal how the unique quality of a place emerges out of the interaction of place and time, such that we can postulate (as the central thesis of this book) that the identity of a community emerges from the successive operations of transformation on a site over time. The site is defined not only by the natural site and all the systems that have produced its unique rock, water, and vegetation patterns, but also by the man-made interventions that inhabit a site. A virgin landscape is as much a "site" as a densely inhabited urban condition.

Contemporary development practices, especially in suburbs, typically favor demolition and erasing records of past natural and human traces, a practice that has left suburban sites with relatively temporally shallow identities. In these cases, the evidence of recorded "time" is muted, (t = 0) and consequently leaves little to distinguish one suburban location from another. The challenge facing suburbs is how to highlight, amplify, and build upon its unique attributes such that their identities evolve, adding temporal depth over time.

Ironically, since the suburbs have accelerated business and residential lifecycles, they have the ability to foster and promote unique identities by selectively capturing and integrating ongoing transformations, as opposed to erasing each iteration of building with each economic cycle. Building with this awareness in mind can allow future iterations of construction (writing) and demolition (erasure) to be carried out in reference to a specific place and time. With this process it is possible that we can create communities which, when viewed by archeologists in thousands of years, might possess the richness of Cologne.

Time as Method, where Time = Reading, Writing, and Erasing

If the Identity = Site + Time equation is true, it follows that "time" is the necessary means by which identity can evolve. But what plans and physical actions comprise the operations of time, operations that can transform the edge? Consider the metaphor of a city as a palimpsest. A palimpsest is defined as a text that has been written upon and erased over time, leaving traces of past writings and erasures. In ancient texts, where the value of the surface written upon was so great that it was simply reused, it is possible to see fragments, imprints, and partial erasures of previous writings and erasures. The text has a temporal depth that is entirely lacking in a computer generated laser print. This definition suggests two critical operations—erasing and writing—but presupposes a third operation, namely that of reading. It is necessary to first read and analyze the text to see that nothing of value is lost before deciding what to erase or write. It follows then that actions that take place over time are those of erasing and writing, or in reverse order, but always proceeded by reading. This iterative process, when executed over an extended period of time, will provide the edge city a temporal depth and emerging identity that it lacks today.

Reading: Gathering, Compiling, Mapping, and Analyzing Information

Reading site like a text operates at multiple levels. One type of reading simply scans what is visible and apparent to all. But a good reader will also try to derive meaning beyond what is immediately visible. For instance, what is the structure of the text, what are the components of its organization, what does it mean, what is the function of the narrative? Like a text, a site should be read first on its surface and secondly in a way that allows its structure and meaning to be better understood. The tools and devices used to understand a reading of an urban or suburban text are maps, corresponding quantitative data, satellite images, and three-dimensional visualizations. These tools can be useful in understanding the physical characteristics of a site—both its man-made features and its natural systems. After assembling the necessary information and data, this information can be dissected so that each set of elements or information can be clustered layer by layer. Maps are the most convenient way of documenting this information, and thanks to advances in computer technologies and graphic methods, it will be possible to highlight and illustrate salient data about the relationships between the many systems that operate on a site, and what they reveal about its deep structure.

Erasing

Erasure is by definition a destructive act. It removes evidence of some previous action or event recorded on an object, field, or text. Erasure is an essential and necessary component in making our environments, allowing them to renew and regenerate their surfaces and structures in order to accommodate new uses and technologies. Without erasure, the residue of history would suffocate communities. Selective erasure can reveal and activate the potential for new and exciting possibilities, like cyclical fires in great forests.

Thus, paradoxically, erasure can be constructive. Take as an example the Boston's central artery, an elevated highway, built in the 1950s, that sliced right through the city's historic core. Its location isolated one neighborhood from another and severed the harbor from the city. Another act of erasure followed, however, namely the removal of the elevated highway, and its replacement with a new underground highway, capable of carrying twice the traffic. The Big Dig as it is called, will enable the rebuilding of demolished and erased historic blocks, thereby stitching together the fabric of the city, its waterfront, and the business district. Any act of erasure should be considered carefully: what will be the consequences of erasing this feature or that and what opportunities does it provide for the future?

List of Operations of Erasure

Eradication (complete)	E_{ce}
Eradication (partial)	E_{pe}
Etching	E_{tc}
Excision	E_{ex}
Entropy	E_{en}
Excavation	E_{ev}

Complete Eradication

The operation of complete eradication removes any and all material from a project site. The degree of "completeness" is defined by site boundaries. Examples of complete eradication are numerous, and on a larger scale include war-torn cities such as Dresden and Hiroshima. Other examples include the demolition of the Pruitt-Igoe housing complex in St. Louis. On a more domestic scale, the suburban phenomenon of "tear downs" demolishes post-war housing stock in favor of "McMansions."

4 E_{ce} Eradication (complete)

Partial Eradication

Like complete eradication, partial eradication removes material from a site, but only certain elements, so that evidence of the site's context and its underlying order are still apparent. The difference between partial and complete eradication is a matter of degree; it involves renovation rather than reconstruction. Voids and scars left by partial eradication beg completion and renewal. The partial eradication in 1976 of the additions that accreted to Boston's Quincy Market allowed the 180-year-old structure to be rejuvenated as a market place.

5 E_{pe} Eradication (partial)

Etching

Etching marks the site, leaving a trace of past interventions or future intentions. This registration can be left through the faint removal of material from a surface, through its chemical transformation (akin to the actual process of etching), or the minimal addition of material to delineate the trace. Examples of etching include the chalk marks of a surveyor on roadways charting the location of infrastructure below the surface. Scrapes and incisions can mark a site's past and future.

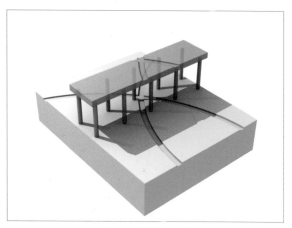

6 E_{tc} Etching

Excision

An excision is a precise and deliberate cut through an existing urban context or building. It slices through a fabric or mass sometimes without full regard for the potential damage it may cause to the integrity of a city and its buildings, their spaces and supporting systems. Excision can also be motivated by the need to liberate, reveal, or explore parts of buildings as well as connect remote or inaccessible points or destinations. An example of excision is Barron Haussmann's Boulevard Rue de Rivoli in Paris, designed to link two remote urban nodes, the Bastille with the Place de la Concorde, both to create new urban connections and to limit the effectiveness of barricading rioters.

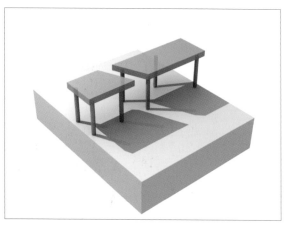

7 E_{ex} Excision

Entropy

The operation of entropy is ever-present as a natural force. It degrades and disintegrates a site's structures. The durability of a buildings lifecycle is a function of the materials used and the method of construction. Without continuous renewal and investment, the forces of nature will break down the structure and its component parts. Any ancient ruin is a testament to the power of entropy.

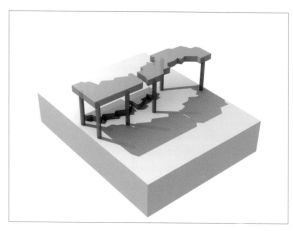

8 E_{en} Entropy

Excavation

Excavation digs into the earth or under buildings. It violates the surface of the current ground plane to reveal or expose previous constructions or new foundations. Excavations are defined by their perimeter and depth, such that new volumes of space are created. Archeologists excavate to reveal past histories, where the depth of the terraced plots mark time in reverse. The miner excavates the earth to extract minerals from its hardened crust. Tunnels bored under rivers and harbors link and connect places divided by water.

9 E_{ev} Excavation

Writing

Where erasure removes material from a site, writing adds or repositions material. Writing is a deliberate act, requiring intent. The intent is to construct, by assembling materials, and components, a structure that defines volume and space for a multitude of residential, private, and public uses. Volumes create space by establishing boundaries. The shape and configuration of boundaries are contingent upon many factors, such as cultural norms, the site configuration, available resources, the program (preferred use), and the constraints of construction systems. The act of writing can be unconscious or conscious, done by individuals or groups. It can be executed with great flourish and energy or with restraint. Physical and cultural contexts can be considered or ignored. There are no limits to the types of writing that can occur on a site. They can be categorized typologically or by formal attributes.

Like erasure, the effects of writing can be paradoxical. That is, poorly considered acts of writing can destroy evidence of past writing and its traces, by acting as a sort of operation of erasure. For instance, the unmitigated effects of urban sprawl have erased traces of the natural landscape. Similarly, the successive acts of building on an ancient tell in present day Iraq, serve to erase evidence of past civilizations. The only clue to the city's past is its elevated profile.

List of Operations of Writing

Parceling	W_p
Infill	W_i
Addition	W_{ad}
Absorption	W_{ab}
Enveloping	W_{en}
Wrapping	W_w
Overlay	W_o
Parasitic	W_{pa}
Morphing	W_m

Parceling

Parceling is often the first act of writing on a site. It defines the territorial boundaries of future acts of writing and erasing. The operation of parceling is not limited to two dimensions but can be stacked three dimensionally, without topological limits. The incredible density of housing units interspersed with shops found in Kowloon,

Hong Kong represents a complexly configured nest of interlocking parceled volumes. The density of parceling reflects the value of land and the volumes it supports. As land becomes more valuable, the grain (size) of parcels tends to become finer, allowing higher unit costs to be supported by increased volume of inhabitants. The average cost of real estate in Cheyenne, Wyoming versus Manhattan, New York reflects this phenomenon. Radical reparceling of land and volumes of space is a function of larger economic forces and the cost of development.

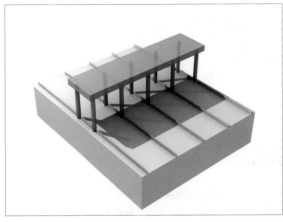

10 W_p Parceling

Infill

Infilling is about filling or constructing a void. The void can be territorial, as in building on a lot that has been parceled. Or infill can also be about filling the gap between two preexisting buildings or structures. Like filling in the space created by a missing tooth, infill is important in creating continuity in our environments. Infill involves taking advantage of existing capacity rather than constructing new infrastructure, and can slow the rate at which rural landscapes and functioning ecosystems are paved over by development.

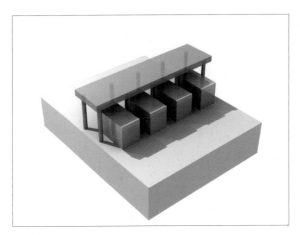

11 W_i Infill

Addition

Addition cannot by definition exist without some preexisting condition (i.e., a structure must occupy an existing parcel to which it can be added). Addition of material is outward or upward from the original form. Boston's Customs House Tower demonstrates how a squat 60-foot high Greek Revival courthouse became the base for what was, for a while, Boston's tallest tower. On a smaller domestic scale, the construction of additions can be found across cultures, as people expand habitable spaces beyond original boundaries.

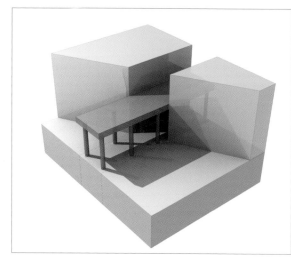

13 W$_{ab}$ Absorption

Enveloping

Enveloping is a more complete and three-dimensional form of absorption, where a structure is entirely enveloped by its surrounding context, so that not even a trace of the original form can be distinguished from the exterior. It is only by moving through a space that the original building and its enveloping volumes can be distinguished. The labyrinthine spaces found in Middle Eastern souks and kasbahs illustrate this phenomenon.

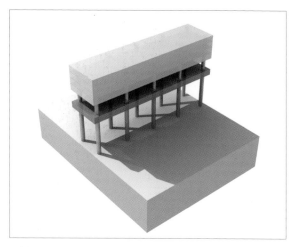

12 W$_{ad}$ Addition

Absorption

Absorption describes the change that occurs when the space around a building or object is encroached upon. The process can be gradual or accelerated, yet in both cases the original object is no longer distinguishable as a separate entity from its surrounding context. The Roman amphitheater in Florence has been absorbed into the urban fabric by 2000 years of urban development, so that its original elliptical plan is only faintly recognizable in aerial photographs.

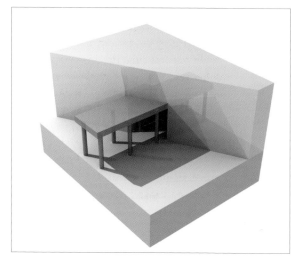

14 W$_{en}$ Enveloping

Wrapping

Wrapping sheathes an existing volume or surface in a new skin, redefining the boundary between the interior and exterior. In the art world, Christo's wrapping of famous artifacts such as Berlin's Reichstag, is an example of wrapping. In construction, old buildings are often reclad in new or dissimilar materials as the lifecycle of building components complete their useful life. Increasingly skyscrapers' exterior envelopes are re-sheathed in new high-performance materials. The depth of the skin need not be limited to the width of a wall, and can entail the creation of thicker, habitable zones of space, wrapping existing volumes.

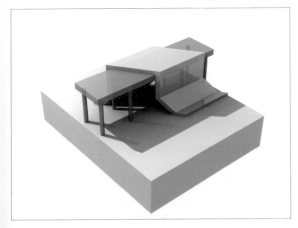

15 W_w Wrapping

Overlay

Where an existing structure needs to retain its form and attachment to the ground plane, a new form or system can be built over the existing structure, sharing its air rights but maintaining the integrity of the structure below. A highway pass is a simple example of one form of infrastructure spatially overlaid onto another without disrupting the operation of either system. Air rights development projects in Seattle, Hong Kong, New York, and Paris, among other cities, demonstrate how different structures and systems can be overlaid as the needs of cities and their services expand in scope and complexity.

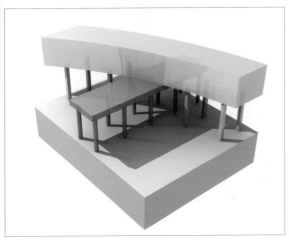

16 W_o Overlay

Parasitic

A larger construction can serve as an armature, or host, to smaller embedded accretions of forms and spaces. As the accretions enlarge in size and form, they gradually overtake the host structure, so that its original form is no longer identifiable. The organic growth patterns of Italian hill towns, where constructed townscapes are deeply rooted to the host landscape, illustrate how built and natural landscapes merge into a new form.

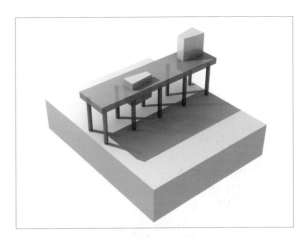

17 W_{pa} Parasitic

Morphing

In morphing, the material and volume of a form remain constant, while its shape and configuration transform and mutate into new forms. Forms may be subtly redefined or radically altered, to the point where the original typology of a building may no longer be visible. The constantly redefined edges of ocean barrier reefs as well as deltas are examples of how the configuration of land is constantly altered. Historic architectural precedents sometimes arise from the erosion of natural forms, as in the case of many southwestern Indian cave dwellings (pueblos). Contemporary examples reflect the power of digital tools to topologically adjust forms to meet design parameters as part of a design process, as well as the application of new pneumatic structures and advanced technologies.

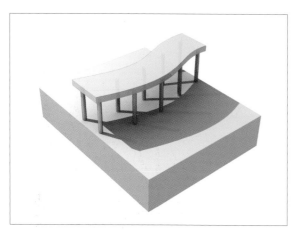

18 W_m Morphing

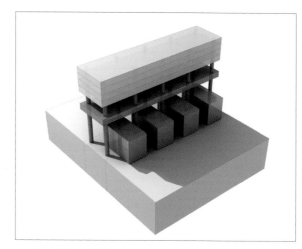

20 W_{ad} Addition + W_i Infill

New Spatial-Temporal Typologies

The operations of erasure and writing, as they are executed on an object, a building, or a city can generate a wide array of new typologies that represent the interaction of an existing typology with time. For instance, a diagram of an elevated bridge undergoing erasure, say excavation (E_{ev}), is then combined with another operation of writing, say overlay (W_o), to create a composite typology. This diagram begins to represent the types of changes that richly layered sites undergo, generating unusual and surprising hybrid typologies. They are unique and particular products of time and circumstance, and contribute to the characteristics that distinguish the identity of one place from another. The various combinations in analyzing existing and new spatial-temporal typologies are infinite in their capacity to create configurations that "fit" the needs of evolving suburban contexts.

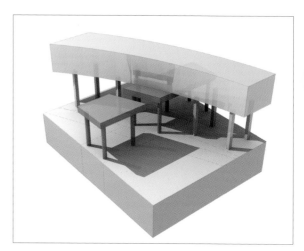

21 W_o Overlay + E_{ex} Excision

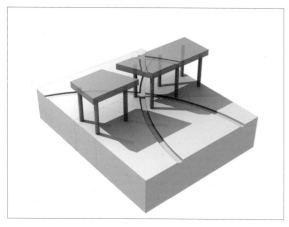

19 E_{ex} Excision + E_{tc} Etching

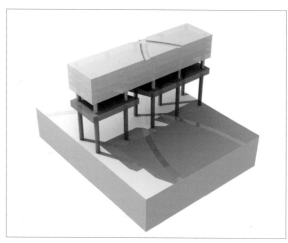

22 E_{ex} Excision + E_{tc} Etching + W_{ad} Addition

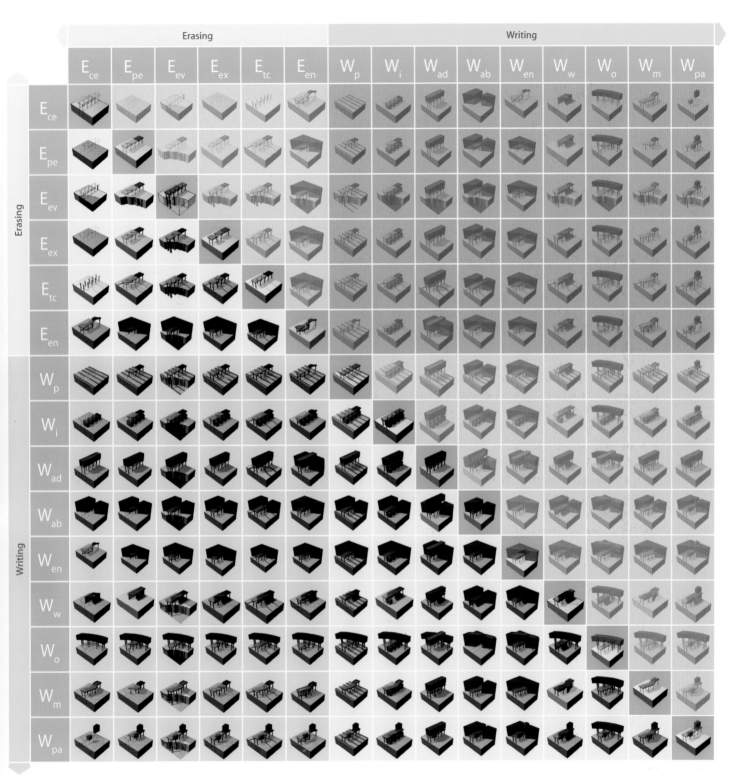

23 Spatial-temporal typologies overlaying operations of erasure and writing

24 Examples of overlaid operations of writing

Illustrating Transformations: Creating Strings

The list of operations above is not intended to be exhaustive or complete; instead it represents a starting point for documenting change. These operations serve as a language or code that can describe the kinds of transformations that have taken place on a building, a space, or a portion of the urban fabric. The operations function at all scales, from that of city, to that of detail. An excision can be cut through a city like Florence, as it can be cut through an interior wall.

In addition, this code of operations can be developed further, to describe in greater specificity the numerous attributes associated with each operation, occurring at a specific instant (t_n). Attributes can include quantitative and qualitative information. Quantitative data such as spatial coordinates, volume of material displaced, and costs can easily be associated with each operation and its temporal coordinates. Similarly, the qualitative attributes of each operation can be described to include representations of the kinds of materials and their formal characteristics. New computer software could be developed to track changes in such detail.

Most promising is the possibility of using this code to describe the history of a site. First, each operation occurring at a particular instant (t_n) can be documented. For example, an operation of *erasure* (say excision E_{ex}) occurring to an object or space, at an instant (t_n), would be recorded as ($E_{ex}t_n$). If one begins to list the multiple sets of operations that have taken place on an object over time, it is possible to document its history as a string of operations, each with its own temporal coordinates. These strings would look like filmstrips, or a repetition of frames showing changes at set intervals of time. Each object in a city could have its own string, such that it would be possible to analyze the potential (causal) relationships between operations, their sequence, and their location for instance. Such an analysis might begin to yield a better understanding of the vagaries of time as something more than random acts. Such a tool would enable designers and developers to design with time.

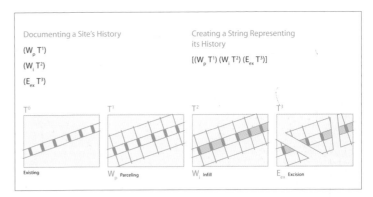

25 A string representing site's history

Harnessing the Forces of Time

Cities that have undergone significant transformations illustrate the rich interplay of space and use, an interplay that defies conventional typological definition. These precedents arise from the particularity of a site and very specific responses to the nature of place and circumstance. The Adaptive Design Process can help a suburban community begin to translate the seemingly happenstance operations of change occurring over time into a coherent process, one that harnesses forces that reinforce, rather than dispel, aspects of site and identity. The Adaptive Design Process is a means through which the force of time can be harnessed to create environments rich in identity. It opens up the design process to time, the information inextricably linked to identity, and the multiple actors that have a stake in the development of a site and its environment.

Opportunities to create new spatial-temporal typologies and harness the forces of time are easy to find, because they are built into any community, system, or structure with components that have varying lifecycles.

Lifecycles

Despite man's heroic attempts to counter the forces of entropy, cities, buildings, and monuments decay. Decay is due to the forces of nature (sunlight, wind, water, chemical decomposition, and natural disaster) as well as the wear caused by man, through inhabitation. Structures can be sustained through ongoing maintenance and renewal of components and their assemblies. The study of building economics examines the relationship of building lifecycles and their economic performance.[1] Buildings are comprised of several clusters of systems, each with its own lifecycle. Depending on the method of construction and culture, these groups might include (from longest lasting to shortest lifecycle): 1) foundations, 2) structure, 3) exterior walls, 4) interior walls, 5) appliances. Each of these lifecycle groups and its elements must be replaced and maintained at a different rate. Thus buildings, if they are sustained, undergo constant transformation. New technologies and improvements on building components, make it possible to improve and alter buildings through the gradual replacement of outdated components, such that the evolving forms of cities and their buildings change gradually, but significantly, over time.

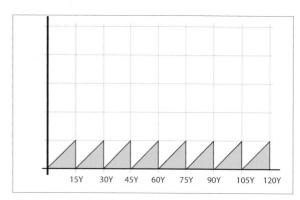

29 Infill, 30 years

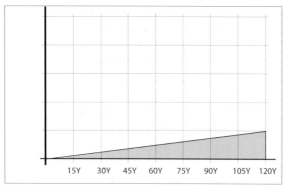

26 Infrastructure life cycle, 120+ years

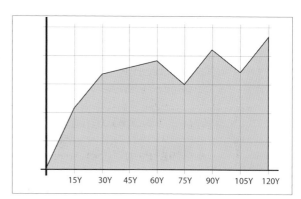

30 Appliances, 15 years

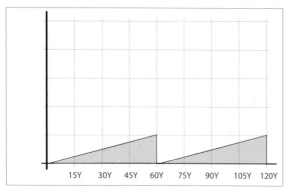

27 Shell life cycle, 60 years

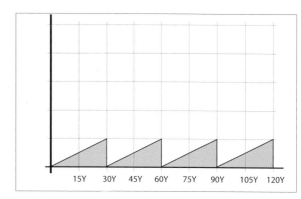

31 Composite

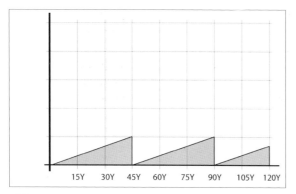

28 Structure, 45 years

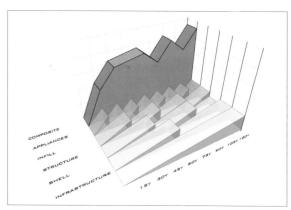

32 Composite graphs

In addition, tax, financial, and development cycles have accelerated significantly over the last fifty years, especially in the commercial and retail sectors. New retail developments are built with projected lifecycles of as little as five years, such that buildings (typically "big boxes") serve an economic purpose in short order and can be discarded.[2] Depreciation cycles and tax laws are continually manipulated to encourage development in certain markets, even if the demand is not present.

Suburban housing developments that exploded in the 1950s have met the limits of their useful lifecycle, and the middle class is abandoning mature "inner suburbs" in many parts of the country. Unable to meet market needs, these suburbs are leapfrogged by larger and newer exurban developments that siphon valuable resources from them. In some places, however, inner suburbs, especially those with attractive amenities, undergo constant renewal through the constant transformation of their housing stock. Units are enlarged, improved, or subdivided into more profitable and economically viable configurations.

If cities, buildings, and their configurations undergo constant change, by virtue of physical and economic necessity, why not take this into consideration in the initial design and construction phases of our communities? The opportunity to minimize waste is well within the limits of our ability to forecast the probable "behavior" of buildings, and the economic and development cycles that generate their shape. We cannot predict the future, but we can work with time as a component of our decision making process. We can also begin to transform existing development as the component systems expire and require replacement.

The Influence of Infrastructure

Infrastructure follows infrastructure. Infrastructure is the backbone of development, and since it is the longest lasting element of the built environment, it can support several waves of development, redefinition, and reordering over time. Infrastructure can play a key role in identifying places, and provides an armature for transformations over time.

Modern societies are defined by mobility. Mobility equals freedom, and freedom is associated with time: time to make money and enjoy the fruits of one's labor. Time also equals convenience. Loss of convenience results in a loss of time, money, and opportunities for recreation. Therefore, the infrastructure of space is the infrastructure of the economy and, by extension, of our culture. The identity of a town, region, state, or country is tied to the shape and form of its infrastructure. Consider how the identity of the TGV is tied to the identity of France, just as the highway is tied to the identity of Los Angeles. Infrastructure serves a functional and economic role as much as it is a symbolic and cultural icon.

Because of its ever-increasing scale, the impact of infrastructure on the shape of our towns and cities is growing. In the same way that Roman aqueducts (their relationship to distant aquifers, angle of incline, and entrance points to the city and its baths) helped determine the viability, capacity, and form of Rome, so do highways (their fluid geometries, expansive width, turning radii, on- and off-ramp design) influence the development of contemporary urban form. For example, the stretches of highway linking Atlanta, Columbia, Charlotte, and Raleigh generate new, smaller communities between the major metropolitan areas that only exist because of the highway itself.

Despite the significance of infrastructure to our societies, remarkably little attention is paid to its form and its influence on the shape of urban areas and surrounding landscapes. New attention must be paid to this long-lifecycle feature of our communities.

What is Infrastructure?

For the purposes of this discussion, infrastructure is divided into two loosely grouped clusters. One cluster focuses on transportation systems, which tend to be publicly accessible and, more often than not, visible. These systems include highways, train lines, waterways, airports, and other forms of transportation networks. The other cluster is based on a distribution of public services and resources. These include, water, sewer, power, and telecommunications. The distribution of these systems is not always visible, and more often than not has limited access. Infrastructure also implies that a common public need is served, and it is usually funded and built by the public sector. (There are, of course, many examples where public-private entities have collaborated on the construction of infrastructure.) Infrastructure can also be built entirely by the private sector, which sells

33 Roman aqueduct hugging Rome's walls

34 High Line cutting through Chelsea, New York City

35 Expressway hovering over Shanghai cityscape

its products and services either to governments or to the public. Oil companies, for example, build extensive networks of pipelines that cross national boundaries. Similarly, private radio and media outlets buy or lease access to public airwaves.

However, the very definition of infrastructure is in constant flux. For instance, isn't a park a form of infrastructure? Similarly, cities often build parking structures to attract businesses and development. Increasingly, the amenities and services required to attract or sustain development are forms of infrastructure, financed and built through public, private, or public-private partnerships. There is also a growing recognition of green infrastructure, or important natural features that provide ecosystem services to society. Forests, for example, retain moisture, stabilize soils, recharge groundwater levels, sequester carbon dioxide from the atmosphere, and provide important wildlife habitat. Wetlands, farms, trails, river corridors, prairies, and estuaries all provide a range of services that benefit society. In the event of rapid and severe climate change, uplands may offer the only refuge for plants and animals that migrate slowly and are unable to outpace rising temperatures by migrating to cooler latitudes.[3]

This book focuses primarily on those man-made infrastructure systems (highways, roadways, train lines, transportation networks, parking, parks, etc.) that are typically found in the immediate vicinity of towns loosely defined as suburbs or edge cities, because, from a design perspective, they have been largely ignored. In addition, suburbs are increasingly attracting larger populations and development. The role that infrastructure plays in supporting and sustaining these developments is critical and must be balanced with the need to sustain the presence of the landscape. Given the strong connection between the identities of our communities and the forms of infrastructure, it is important to find ways in which the shape, configuration, and location of infrastructure can help evolve the identities of our communities.

Many examples illustrate how infrastructure could shape a community's identity. The Italian futurists like Sant'Elia produced magnificent representations of urban complexes built around speed and mobility. Between the world wars, architects like Harvey Wiley Corbett and Raymond Hood developed fantastic proposals for integrating buildings with highways and bridges (Towers on the Hudson River Bridge). New York-based artist Hugh Ferris carved in charcoal crystalline forms representing the evolution of skyscrapers based on zoning laws, light, and the flow of traffic. The 1964 New York World's Fair displayed a spectacular model (sponsored by General Motors) of the city of the future, replete with multi-level integrated pedestrian and auto traffic systems. Louis Costa's design of Brasilia is, of course, the embodiment of infrastructure as city. More recently, and on a more modest scale, Lady Bird Johnson spearheaded a program to beautify the long stretches of highway throughout Texas with landscape improvements. While some of the above noted examples take extreme positions relative to the role of infrastructure in shaping our environment, each considers it in a deliberate fashion, not as a haphazardly designed component of the landscape, but one that is fully integrated in its context.

The result of failing to consider the form and shape of infrastructure elements visible in the environment is potentially damaging to the landscape and existing settlements. Where highway standards for optimal inclines and radii dictate preferred geometries, natural landscape features and towns are bulldozed with little regard for the consequences to the shape of the land.

Singularly focused highway design strategies disregard how the highway meets existing towns, complexes, or buildings, resulting in an enormous amount of "leftover" space between the highway and adjacent buildings and sites. The "space between" the highway and neighboring buildings and cities is often ill-defined, having no discernable shape. Such spaces are characteristic of communities without strong identities. Consider the compelling identity of Parisian four- to eight-lane boulevards, bounded by a continuous row of mature trees, which in turn shelters pedestrians and patrons of local cafes sipping Chardonnay. The road engages automobile and pedestrian alike, and the shapes of the street, buildings, trees, and sidewalks are integrated to create a pleasing experience. Such is the role that infrastructure can play; it is the armature for transformation.

Endnotes

1   For a more detailed account of building lifecycles, see Stewart Brand, *How Buildings Learn*.

2   Wal-Mart is infamous for building enormous retail centers on the outskirts of small towns, in effect destroying existing "main street" retail and then fleeing to greener pastures in several years, leaving a retail, economic, and social void.

3   Gretchen Daily and Katherin Ellison, *New Economy of Nature: The Quest to Make Conservation Profitable* (Washington, D.C.: Island Press, 2002). Also see Mark Benedict and Ed McMahon, *Green Infrastructure: Linking Landscapes and Communities* (Washington, D.C.: Island Press, 2006), 12.

The Adaptive Design Process

The current mode of development and construction is based on a highly compressed design and construction schedule. Developers, retailers, and institutions identify a window of opportunity, determined in part by available financing and market demand. Consequently, once the decision has been made to proceed, design and development are propelled through the review and construction process. Because of tight economic margins, developments often rely on set typologies for office and retail construction. The undifferentiated reuse of these typologies contributes to the uniform appearance of so many edge-city conditions. Buildings are plopped onto sites, with less concern for the creation of habitable and unique environments, than with working within parking, zoning, and economic parameters. The current process is geared toward meeting the exigencies of today, with little regard for the latent identity of a site and the impact and promise current developments bring to its future. There is no latitude for temporal depth. The aim of the Adaptive Design Process is to create a process that works within the demands of current markets and economies but considers the past and future.

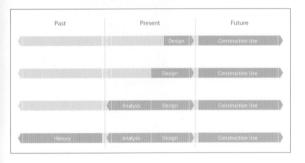

1

The Process

More explicit and reflective about the present condition than other methods, the Adaptive Design Process can bridge past actions with future possibilities. It does so by reassessing conventional design processes as they occur in the present, breaking the process down into six explicitly articulated phases:

→ Mapping
→ Editing
→ Selecting Tools and Typologies
→ Projecting
→ Simulating
→ Recalibrating

MAPPING

The Adaptive Design Process begins with the creation of an extensive database of the site in the form of maps. An enormous array of information from a variety of sources—charts, graphs, quantitative information, site history, natural forces, building histories—all can be translated into the form of a map, thereby creating a consistent visual system through which data about a site can be revealed, analyzed, and interpreted. Mapping is the critical link between the past and the present. Mapping can tell us more about how all the forces acting on a site are affecting current conditions or "behavior." The process of mapping breaks down and represents forces or phenomena into a singular set of conditions.

Premapping

Premapping is the first step in design and helps determine which maps are most likely to yield useful information. Preliminary research can generate valuable information about a site, its history, and political and economic forces. This helps in deciding which maps are more likely to generate useful information. Interviewing local stakeholders (residents and business owners), purveying local publications, and direct site documentation and observation can offer valuable clues in identifying salient issues, and phenomena that may reveal more about the character of a community, its natural, historical, and demographic features.

Mapping History

History documents the significant transformations of a site over time. Perhaps the street pattern has a compelling historical origin. Or the original settlement was destroyed by flooding or fire. The insertion of major infrastructure elements may have caused significant changes in topography or landscape. Or the construction of major buildings and institutions might have fundamentally altered the nature of the community. Historical maps create a narrative about a place and identify the features that make it unique.

Mapping Site Forces

There is no limit to the types of information or phenomena that can be recorded about a site. Site forces range from historical to economic. Some forces are physically apparent, like natural systems (hydrology, topography, geology, vegetation, and climate), infrastructure elements,

Past

History

Present

Analysis

Mapping	Editing
Pre-Mapping	Distilling A Site's "Useful History"
Mapping History	Engagements of History's Residue
	Specific vs. Generic Designs
Mapping Site Forces	Flexible Structural System
Natural Systems	Separation of Lifecycle Assemblies
Infrastructure	Location
Ownership/Control	Perceived Value
Zoning	Engaging History's Traces
Programming	
Buildings	Evaluating Site Forces
Capital Flows	
Sensory Reading	Assessing Community Values
Surfaces	
Statistical	
Cross-Mapping	

T^{-8} T^{-7} T^{-6} T^{-5} T^{-4} T^{-3} T^{-2} T^{-1}

2 Diagram of the Adaptive Design Process

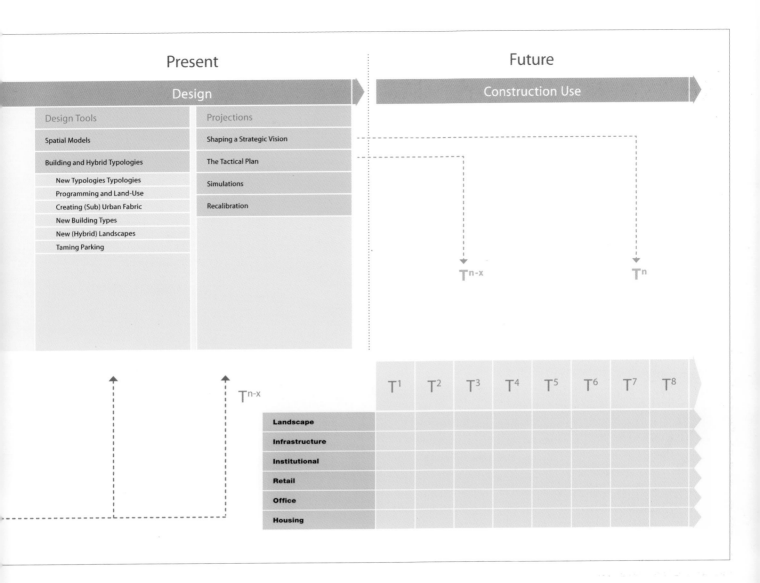

3 GIS data: Percent of owner occupied homes in the Boston metropolitan area

Percent Owner Occupied
0-25%
26-50%
51-75%
75-90%
91-100%
No Data

(highways, bridges, or rail lines), or buildings (a site's building typologies, construction types, materials, and structural systems). Other forces may be legal or demographic, including ownership, zoning, programming or capital flows. Sensory readings record the sensory information available at any site, including audio, olfactory, tactile, and visual attributes. Visual attributes might include sight lines as one moves across a site, the legibility of figural spaces, as well as lighting levels. Noise readings can be charted for points across a site, to identify effects of major sound sources: airplanes following a flight path overhead or trucks thundering down the highway. Smells of industry, nature, and food can be interpreted and mapped. *Statistical maps* can reveal many quantifiable attributes representing critical information such as demographics, traffic counts, or air quality. GIS data can greatly enhance understanding of complex communities.

Cross-Mapping

The forms of most human settlements arise out of a confluence of natural and man-made forces over time. The resulting elements rarely demonstrate a consistent hierarchical set of relationships. Even in environments where a strong set of principles govern development— Savannah, Georgia, for instance, or Bern, Switzerland— one can observe places where the order breaks down, typically in response to a constraint defined by a natural system like a river's edge, which disrupts a perfect grid pattern, or historic circumstances such as the insertion of a larger bridge required to support heavier traffic. Cross-mapping reveals and confirms the existence of

hierarchies, conflicts, opportunities, and problems. It is literally an overlaying of one map onto another to observe and analyze the relationships and disparities between the forces existing on the site. An entire chapter in this book is devoted to cross-mapping to demonstrate its visual power and interpretive possibilities.

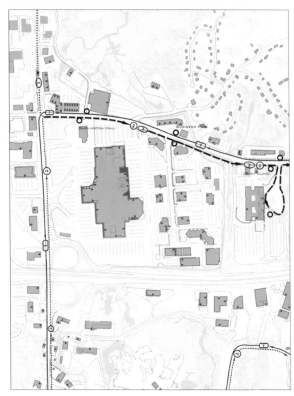

4 Cross-map of bus routes vs. pedestrian routes in Burlington, Massachusetts

EDITING

The mapping process generates vast amounts of information about the site while revealing factors that contribute to its identity. It is important that a set of criteria be in place through which this information can be filtered and evaluated. The editing process is an effort to organize information toward the shaping of future design proposals.

Distilling a Site's "Useful History"

A site's built history should be as fully engaged as possible in future developments. Analyzing the usefulness of existing elements will reveal both their potential for transformation as well as their significance in relation to a site's unique identity. Reuse and rehabilitation of existing structures represents the primary way through which history can be actively engaged. The generic quality of many existing structures allows them to be used differently over time, enhancing their chances for survival. Without thinking about time, resources can be wasted through the frequent cycles of building and demolition particularly evident in commercial and retail construction. For instance, many suburbs witness the quick construction of buildings, such as retail centers, which are torn down only to be replaced by larger structures. These new structures sometimes share the same type of structural systems as the original buildings. Far better it would be to reuse original structures, in part or in whole, provided original designs fit current needs. Often contractors and developers do not proceed with this option, because either the original design does not fit the needs or because labor costs dictate that simply tearing a building down and rebuilding from scratch is simpler and less expensive. As global competition for resources becomes greater with time, this equation may change, such that saving resources will be economically beneficial.

A number of factors contribute to the likelihood that a building can be reused in the future for similar or different uses:

Specific vs. Generic Designs

The degree of specificity that a building is configured to meet particular program needs, impacts its ability to be readily transformed for other uses. That is, the more specifically a building's walls, openings, roofs, etc. are designed to meet a particular need (a private residence, church, or library) the less likely it is that the structure will be able to accommodate a new use. Conversely, more generic buildings, such as warehouses, industrial buildings, and marketplaces, lend themselves to a multitude of adaptive reuses. That is why, for instance, so many school buildings have been converted to condominium housing units. The regular room sizes and large expansive structural spans allow for greater flexibility in converting spaces to alternate uses.

5 Warehouses that have been expanded into housing at Mockingbird Station, outside Houston, Texas. Courtesy of RTKL.

Flexible Structural System

Generic buildings are more likely to be linked to flexible structural systems, but not always. What is meant by a flexible structural system? It is one that allows for alterations to its uses without major alterations to primary structural support systems (such as principle columns, trusses, and floor assemblies, etc.) For instance, a factory, with a long span structure is an excellent example of a construction that can support a variety of uses without completely reconfiguring their framework. Flexible systems typically have a repetitive structural system, using equal bays and elements. Nineteenth century industrial and mill buildings provide excellent examples, allowing for easy conversion to residences and offices.

Separation of Lifecycle Assemblies

Structures can be designed that are comprised of distinct "lifecycle groups," that is, assemblies of building components sharing lifecycle characteristics. Most speculative office buildings are based on this concept. The shell and structure of a building have one lifecycle (sixty years plus), while the interior walls and partitioning systems have a much shorter lifecycle (about fifteen years). By preconfiguring these buildings into lifecycle groups, it is possible for the assemblies of shorter durations to be ripped out without destroying the structure. In other words, structures can be designed to anticipate the types of uses that might occupy them in the future, and they can be designed such that their structural and building systems are more likely to accommodate changes while working within optimal financing and lifecycle frequencies.

Location, Location, Location

A building might have a very adaptive structure, but if it is positioned against the "grain" of an evolving community, it may fall victim to demolition. For instance, primary traffic patterns might run north and south in a community. While most buildings may be oriented parallel to the north-south axis, one very long structure runs east-west. As the town grows, and needs more roads, the building's contrary orientation may allow it to fall victim to demolition. This occurred, for instance, in the redevelopment of Boston's Waterfront in the 1960s onwards. The large wharf structures that were oriented parallel with the flow of pedestrian and vehicular traffic (from city center to waterfront) survived and were renovated. Those large warehouse structures that were perpendicular to the dominant flow were more likely to be torn down.

Perceived Value

Every building and its components need to be maintained and replaced incrementally over time. If a building has an anticipated 100-year lifecycle, on average 1 percent will be replaced each year. At the end of its useful life, that is, when the building no longer generates an economic return equal to or exceeding its operating expenses, a building will fall into disrepair. There are buildings, though, that for cultural or other reasons generate value outside of conventional economic calculations. These buildings are primarily religious or cultural institutions and can be sustained through subsidies or patronage.

Engaging History's Traces

The remnants of past interventions, such as old railroad beds or foundations, are imbued with meaning. Selectively referencing these traces through new construction can contribute to generating a powerful and unique identity for a community, by reinforcing links between past actions and future intentions.

Evaluating Site Forces

Once the cross-maps have been generated, observations about their content can be organized thematically (category by category), and hierarchically, in order of importance. Cross-maps yielding information of secondary importance can be ignored or discarded. These observations, and their distillation, are a critical act of design, in that they identify themes that serve as the springboard for design proposals.

Assessing Community Values

It is essential to determine a community's values and how these values shape visions for the future. It can be argued that the construction of the community as built is in fact an accurate representation of its values, since the structures built and decisions about land use are determined in part by community representatives. But are edge cities and their attendant problems and negative associations a true reflection of what a citizenry and its representatives desire for their community? Economic interests may or may not balance collective long-term interests with the immediacy of current individual and community needs. A wide-ranging effort to assess community interests and values would include investigating planning reports and surveys; tracking public debates, community activism, and local marketplaces; attending town meetings; and holding community-wide charrettes and creating web related surveys and forums.

SELECTING DESIGN TOOLS

Design tools consist of building typologies, spatial models, and conceptual frameworks that offer mechanisms for translating raw data into coherent design proposals. It is important to select the right tools for transforming a site. Mapping and cross-mapping a site's features and understanding a community's values tell us whether a certain typology or spatial model is suitable.

Building Typologies and Hybrids:

New Infrastructure Typologies

Infrastructure and its adjacent spaces are vastly underutilized in the American suburban landscape. By evaluating the land use of the space on either side and above or below infrastructure, it is possible to increase the value of infrastructure and the land it occupies. Buildings and landscapes can be fused with different forms of infrastructure to create hybrid typologies. Infrastructure can also serve as a buffer, and container, for urban form or landscape.

Programming and Land-Use Strategies

Transforming the edge city and its context into more habitable and sustainable environments will require radically redefining land-use strategies. Considered over a longer time frame, it is possible to redistribute building mass. As buildings decay and fall out of use, those that do not have a "useful history" can be rebuilt in locations that support community objectives, while a strong landscape presence is reestablished in other locations.

Creating Suburban Fabric

Connections between people and the spaces that support their activities define community. However, the edge city and its context, is typically comprised of isolated and disconnected buildings, spaces, and clusters thereof. To create community, it is helpful to generate new kinds of public spaces. Through an incremental process of erasure and writing, connections between buildings and public spaces can be stitched out of an emerging suburban fabric.

New Building Types

The development of new digital technologies allows buildings to perform many different functions in addition to their traditional uses. Emerging e-buildings offer new possibilities for the organization of suburban space and its ability to provide greater efficiency with fewer resources. For instance, e-tailers, who have optimized the distribution of resources, are developing typologies that combine the best features of traditional retail spaces with electronic distribution systems. The management of limited resources can also be improved by timesharing. This allows school buildings, day care centers, and community theaters, for example, to serve multiple uses during the course of the day, week, or month.

New (Hybrid) Landscape Typologies

The desecration of the landscape resulting from the suburban settlement patterns calls for its reconstitution. Landscape presence can be asserted through restoration of a lost landscape, construction of a new landscape, or, where necessary, building an "artificial landscape," which is a new kind of terra firma capable of supporting other uses. Similarly, landscapes constructed as berms can serve conventional building uses, but can also contribute to the landscape as "green" surfaces. Buildings of all kinds can become ubiquitously "green" such that the landscape runs over, through, and under their profiles.

Taming Parking

Parking management remains one of the most difficult problems facing the land-use patterns of suburbs and their edge cities. Accepting the fact that the car will be with us in one form or another, what options exist for reducing its footprint, or mitigating the unsightliness of fields of asphalt parking? Moshe Safdie suggests a form of compressed parking lots, while green urbanists provide a wide array of options for taming parking through landscaping and parking structures that are integral to buildings.[1]

Community Spatial Models

A spatial model serves as an overriding design guideline capable of governing or influencing larger decisions about how and where buildings, spaces, roads, landscape, and infrastructure are organized across a community. Each spatial model is based on a set of principles, objectives, geometries, or collection of building types. The spatial model is an abstract and pure form, providing a hierarchy for urban organization. Grids and radial plans represent classical precedents of spatial forms.

Generating a variety of community spatial models opens up many conceptual avenues for how a site can be developed and organized. As an idealized type, it too, will undergo transformation once it is overlaid onto the complexities and contradictions present in each site. The transformation of idealized community spatial models generates the idiosyncratic qualities of place. For example, idiosyncratic moments happen where Manhattan's generic grid accommodates the slashing cut of Broadway, or the carving out of Central Park.

PROJECTIONS

While most consumer products are designed for a specific moment, community design must consider the element of time. A community is a dynamic living system that supports the lives of its citizenry and their changing needs. Additionally, the very economic structure and social fabric of a community may be in flux. How can design proceed when there are so many variables? What resources and tools might be available in the future, and how might they be incorporated? What if the needs of a community change before a proposal is built?

Projections must be made to anticipate future needs and allow for changing circumstances. The projection phase consists of four steps: 1) shaping a vision, 2) developing plans, 3) simulating results, and 4) recalibrating plans as circumstances change.

A community must be willing to imagine an ideal representation of itself in the future, one that is an outgrowth of its current and desired identity, one distinguishable from its neighbors yet linked to a regional network of similar communities. This is an opportunity to dream, for without ambitious aspirations, it will be difficult for a community to consciously redirect the inertia of past policies and practices. This dream is translated into a "strategic vision," which is a collective and explicit articulation of what a community is to become at some future date. It accounts not just for land-use preferences and social and economic objectives, but also for how these objectives may be manifested in physical form, without necessarily specifically designing each structure or landscape feature.

This strategic vision is accomplished through "tactical" plans. A tactical plan defines the steps that must be executed in order to achieve the larger strategic goals. This can be achieved by breaking down a project's

implementation into phases or "time frames" not unlike the individual frames of a filmstrip.[2] So, for instance, a strategic vision for some twenty-five years in the future could be broken down into twenty-five time frames, illustrating actions required to bring about the desired changes in each year.

It may be useful to break down the investment of physical resources into the categories describing the physical environment. Andres Duany and Elizabeth Plater-Zyberk, in *Suburban Nation*, observe that the suburban environment is comprised of five distinct categories of land uses: Infrastructure, Institutional, Retail, Office, and Housing.[3] One important omission is Landscape. Zoning these separately over the past sixty years has created the very suburbs and edge cities that are in great need of repair. The Adaptive Design Process requires that we mix these components in ways that are particularly suited to site. Rather than separating them spatially, it may be useful to separate them temporally. For instance, an early investment in infrastructure (a high-speed bus service for instance) might spur development around transit locations. Or creating new multi-family housing for local office complexes (which might mitigate traffic) will in turn require institutional investments in larger schools. By breaking down the tactical plans into specific investments, it is possible to coordinate development through time and plan catalytic effects.

Simulations

The matrix described above is also an effective tool for evaluating the probable and actual effectiveness of strategic and tactical plans. By using time-phased "simulations" it is possible to test the results generated by specific tactical plans generated in the service of a strategic plan. Simulations project a series of design transformations, over multiple time frames, showing how a place can be transformed from its existing condition to something that represents a community's strategic vision. A computer model showing incremental changes in the future is useful in illustrating the transformation of a community. The physical elements represented by the computer model can also be linked to sets of attributes. These attributes can be linked to information about a building's economic, engineering, environmental, and demographic information. Cumulatively, such an integrated model serves as a collective database for a site.

Simulations generated by computer models allow communities to evaluate the likelihood of certain tactical plans to meet the stated strategic objectives. This process provides a means for testing the designs before they are built. The simulations are especially useful in testing the sequencing of different investments in different categories (infrastructure vs. institutional). For example (as noted in the previously sited example), at what point should schools or infrastructure be built to support a community's increased population, and what are the economic consequences of these decisions? Will the tax base be big enough to support such investments?

Recalibration

The best-laid plans are rarely carried out as imagined for a multitude of reasons. Design compromises may be required as budgets and available resources change. The demand for specific uses and markets shift in response to demographic and macro-economic changes. Significant historic events, such as, war, energy crisis, or technological revolutions, can completely alter the assumptions that generated a community's original strategic vision. That is why the Adaptive Design Process favors flexible structures and building typologies that can accommodate change, balanced by timeless values represented in the shape of a community's public realm, its open spaces, natural features, and institutions. Missteps are to be expected, but through thoughtful and incremental erasure or writing, remedies can be tested and found for any challenge facing a community.

Strategic plans are most effective when they are dynamic representations of a community's condition and aspirations through time. Being able to respond to changing circumstances will be easier if each member of the community has information at hand regarding its current condition. This can be achieved by continually "updating" the "community database" at each "time frame." As new structures or landscapes are built, this information can be integrated into an evolving representation of the community. The updated community database also offers communities new opportunities and challenges in an informed and timely fashion.

Conclusion

The Adaptive Design Process serves as a useful tool in allowing communities to more explicitly define their current and desired identity and the steps required to achieve these goals. It does so by recognizing that design is an iterative process of erasure and writing.

The Adaptive Design Process serves as an "operating system" of sorts for the development of suburban context. It provides an open and dynamic platform, capable of accommodating a wide array of information, stakeholders, and contexts. As an instrument for change, it is not meant to be prescriptive, but instead capable of itself mutating into variants based on specific needs and circumstances.

As its central structural principle, it builds on time as the means of linking data, design, and experience as communities seek to find the fit between their community's form and its intended use, and all its associations. While the individual steps such as cross-mapping or distilling a site's useful history may improve any design process, Adaptive Design is more effective when the entire process is employed.

This process is not meant to impede spontaneous and idiosyncratic actions that break the rules or evolutionary trends. Instead, it serves as a means of recording, registering, and reminding stakeholders of consequences and opportunities implicit in their actions. Mindful and informed decision-making improves the chance of building thoughtfully conceived environments. The balanced application of analytical tools provided by this process is capable of generating well-tempered environments, by embracing unusual circumstance and the accidents of history, so as to enrich the identity of a place.

Endnotes

1   Moshe Safdie with Wendy Kohn, *The City after the Automobile: An Architect's Vision* (New York: Basic Books, 1998), 142.

2   Walter Benjamin describes the power of film, by saying: "Couldn't an exciting film be made from the map of Paris? From the unfolding of its various aspects in temporal succession? From the compression of a centuries-long movement of streets, boulevards, arcades, and squares into the space of half an hour? And does the flaneur do anything different?" See Convolute, *Ancient Paris, Catacombs, Demolitions, Decline of Paris*, 83.

3   See Andres Duany, Elizabeth Plater-Zyberk, and Jeff Speck, *Suburban Nation: The Rise of Sprawl and the Decline of the American Dream* (New York: North Point Press, 2000), 5.

Chapter 3

Mapping

Burlington is the quintessential edge city, built adjacent to a major highway circumscribing Boston's metropolitan area. Its once bucolic landscape has been transplanted with expansive parking lots, nondescript office complexes, malls, retail centers, entertainment centers, and a collection of service buildings. It is as generic as an edge city can be, and yet it possesses its own rich attributes which could inform future transformations. The following chapters document the speculative transformation of Burlington using the Adaptive Design Process. They explicate the various steps: mapping, cross-mapping, editing, selecting typologies and tools, creating spatial maps, and projecting into the future, using this edge city as a model.

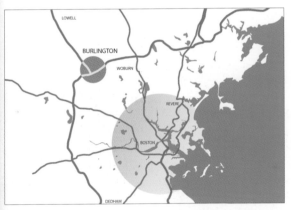

1 Burlington, Massachusetts

A Short History of Burlington

First explored and settled in 1640, Burlington was not incorporated as a town until 1799. It was a place between places, Lexington and Woburn, both of which were larger and more significant. As a resting stop along the stagecoach route, Burlington's early settlement pattern in the eighteenth century clustered along Middlesex Turnpike. This northwesterly route expanded with the onset of the Industrial Revolution. When Lowell emerged in the late 1800s as a major manufacturing center of cloth, Burlington retained its bucolic setting and by 1920 its population was only 1,000.

Its gently rolling hills, forests, farms, fields, irrigated by streams and wetlands, remained as they were for hundreds of years, until the 1950s when two major highways forever changed Burlington's topography and character. The construction of Route 128, the beltway that circumscribes Boston and its suburbs, put Burlington on the map. Route 3 followed, connecting Lowell and New Hampshire in the north to Route 128. Offset by a couple hundred yards, Route 3 runs parallel to the old Middlesex Turnpike. Originally planned to continue south through Lexington, it was abruptly truncated at its intersection with Route 128, thanks to well-organized opposition by the wealthier and more powerful residents of Lexington. Similarly, a proposal to extend Boston's subway line to meet Burlington was rejected, for fear that it would depress land values and that the wrong "elements" might have easy access to peaceful bedroom communities.

At the nexus of intertwining traffic systems, Burlington was ideally situated to exploit its location. Its

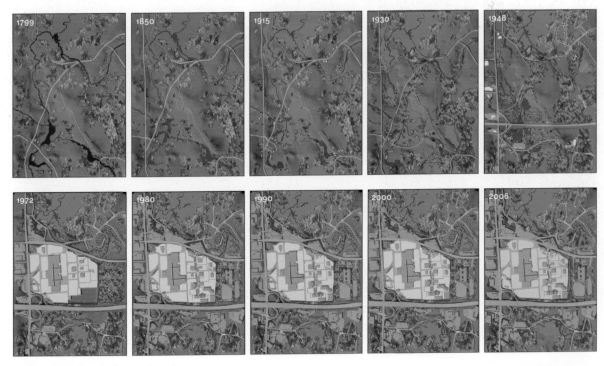

2 Burlington's transformation from 1799 to 2006

population grew from 3,500 in 1950 to 24,000 in 1970. Yet this increase does not adequately reflect the extent of Burlington's growth as a major office and retail center. A feeding frenzy resulted among developers and corporations, as the town offered favorable tax rates to attract development. The Burlington Mall was built in 1968. Its location was so favorable that the owners, the Simon Property Group (currently known as Melvin Simon and Associates) undertook a massive expansion in 1982, adding a new floor and extending the perimeter of the mall's boundary. In 2006, major corporate retail giants emerged necessitating corporate restructuring of assets. Consequently the spaces allocated for anchor tenants like Filene's are being transformed through major renovations. Even today, the Burlington Mall is among the most profitable malls in the United States based on revenues generated per square foot.

Town planners saw aggressive development as a way to increase the town's tax base. Generously subsidized by business interests, the residents' tax burden would be presumably reduced. The reality of this assumption has, however, not been realized, since today this small town of 23,000 residents finds that its infrastructure and services must support an additional 40,000 office workers and hordes of shoppers. As a major regional retail and business center its population can swell from between 70,000 and 140,000 people per day, especially during holiday shopping seasons, when finding a parking space in the mall's parking lot is difficult at best.

Today, the two-mile-long, one-mile-wide stretch of development along the highway is occupied by an array of uses including retail, office, and health-related industries. The Lahey Clinic, world renowned for its cancer treatments, is the largest employer, with over 3,500 staff members. High-tech companies such as Sun Micro Systems, Siemens Nixdorf, Raytheon, Oracle, Hewlett-Packard, Nokia, and many start-up companies have based their corporate facilities here. With this concentration of tech development, Burlington is a bicoastal satellite to Silicon Valley, with employees shuttling back and forth for stays averaging a week or longer. Many corporations rent out entire floors year round at local hotels. Shopping opportunities abound for these workers, but dining, entertainment, and recreation and cultural opportunities are more limited.

According to the 2000 Census report conducted by the U.S. Census Bureau, the average income per capita is $42,562, while the median housing cost for a single family home is $420,400. With over 8,400 housing units, its average household size is just under three persons per unit. The town is experiencing both an elderly and school-aged population boom, creating a greater demand on services (schools, playing fields, etc.) along with a reduced capacity to pay for these services as the incomes of the town's retired population flattens.

Housing is spatially segregated and largely confined outside the perimeter of commercial development, creating in some ways two distinct communities within a town. Single-family dwelling units make up the majority of the housing stock, except for a limited number of multi-family units close to the retail and office complexes. Tract homes are organized around the classic subdivision patterns of romantically conceived streets terminating in cul-de-sacs.

The town's identity is admittedly schizophrenic, part historic bedroom community, part bustling edge city. The town residents benefit from the tax benefits provided by the an edge city's successful businesses, without sacrificing the quest for the American Dream—a house in a pastoral setting. But the financial benefits do not come without a price, as asphalt parking fields compromise its landscape. The town is desperately trying to assert its identity by creating the symbols of community as it reconstitutes its historic "common," like those found in historic neighboring towns such as Lexington and Concord. Yet, the question arises: What is the true identity of Burlington? A facsimile of a quaint New England village, or an economically dynamic, albeit poorly designed edge city? How might these opposing tendencies be reconciled within the limits of contemporary economies?

Natural Systems

The site's natural features, as they appear today, can be dissected system by system. This process illuminates the site's topography, geology, hydrology, and vegetation patterns. Topography could also be profiled in cross-section to reveal the slope of the land.

3 Topography

4 Geology

Topography

Burlington is positioned as a regional crest, with an average peak elevation of 220 feet above sea level. The Ice Age played an important role in shaping the drumlins, or rolling hills and valleys found in the region. Their elongated axis is north-south. Man brought about later topographic transformations, as wetlands and their depressions were filled. Turnpikes and highways carve, berm, and buttress land to create lanes expeditious for travel.

Geology

Burlington's geology shadows its topography. The profiles of the drumlins carry glacial deposits. Deposits occurred in locations where the underlying rock formations and the physics of glacial movement created repositories for glacial till. The land between drumlins allows for the movement of water (above and below grade) through sandy soil.

Soil Limitations

Soil relates to the site's geology. The Lahey Clinic sits atop solid rock, while the inexpensively constructed retail and office complexes sit on fill. Interestingly, the highway runs mostly along solid ground, revealing the engineers' careful analysis of the site and its capacity for underpinning infrastructure.

Its relatively high elevation allows the region to serve as a watershed for three important rivers: the Mystic, the Ipswich, and Shawsheen. Because each of these rivers flows in a different direction, they historically provided water access to several neighboring towns. A number of secondary waterways such as Vine Brook, a north-south tributary of the Shawsheen River, also occupy the site. Vine Brook, which runs through the commercial developments neighboring Route 128, was clumsily redirected to make room for the mall and the office park.

6 Aquifer

Aquifer

The most important aquifer is located right below the mall's parking lot, where oil, salt, and debris collect and seep into the ground.

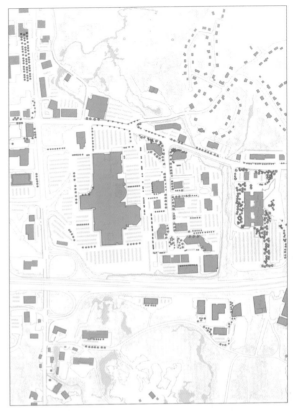

7 Man-made vegetation (plantings)

8 Natural vegetation

Vegetation

The site's natural vegetation patterns range from the swampy valleys of Great Meadow and Long Meadow to the heavily wooded slopes of Burlington's hills. Stone walls created by early settlers and farmers are still evident.

Infrastructure

Burlington's development has been highly dependent on infrastructure systems, some visible, others less prominent or hidden. Paths, roads, and highways all played important roles in shaping Burlington. Less visible (but equally important) forms of infrastructure such as power and sewer lines crisscross the landscape. Data and telecommunications lines, the lifeblood of contemporary corporations, represent significant investments in Burlington's current infrastructure.

Roads

The network of roads is dominated by large arteries (the highway, Middlesex Turnpike, and Mall Road). Secondary and tertiary roads are infrequent and serve only single areas. Links are rare as are networks of smaller roads.

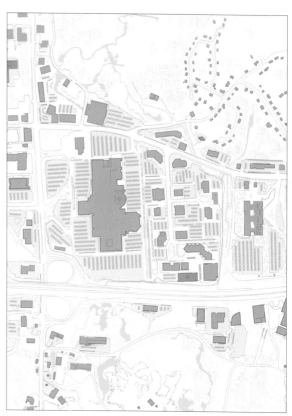

10 Parking

Parking

Parking lots come in all shapes and sizes, but tend to maximize number of cars parked. Simple geometry (square or rectangle) makes for a more efficient layout.

Pedestrian Sidewalks

Sidewalks are randomly placed. Longer runs of sidewalks are disconnected. Only along Mall Road and the office park do they begin to create a continuous pedestrian system.

9 Roads

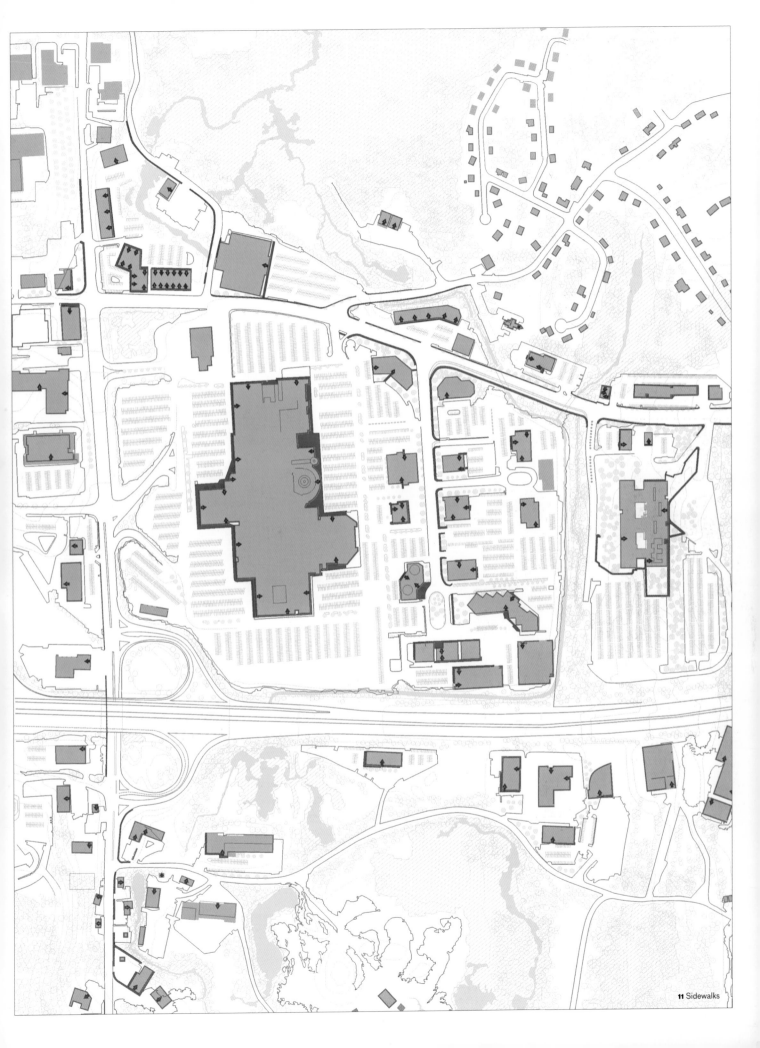

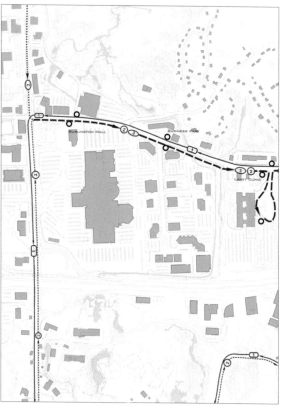

12 Bus routes

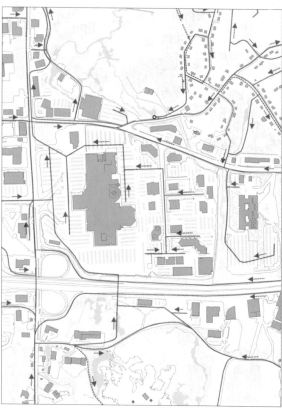

13 Sewer lines

Tenuous transit connections link Burlington Mall to the town center and neighboring Lexington, Arlington, and Woburn. Bus routes loop the mall's parking lot along Middlesex Turnpike and Mall Road and service office complexes, hotels, and the clinic. Schedules are infrequent and stops inconveniently located.

The logic of civil engineering dictates that principal sewer lines should follow primary roads and arteries, providing easy access for future repairs. However, major developments like the mall, the office complex, and the Lahey Clinic have their own independent routes, off the primary roads. Building new developments along existing roads and sewer lines can eliminate the need for costly infrastructure expenditures.

Ownership

Where the private sector plays a significant role in development, land ownership patterns often dictate or influence the shape of future settlements. During the agricultural era the shape of land plots was generated in part by the site's topography, soil, and access to markets. Land deals and swaps made throughout the years between different landowners created unusual plot configurations. After World War II, rampant land speculation began to reconfigure land holdings. Parcel shapes were influenced by anticipated value generated by preferred access to roadways and zoning regulations. Given the past "discretionary zoning" practices of Burlington's town planning arm, the rhyme or reason for many of its parcels is discernable to those with a fine-tuned understanding of the complex legal and financial constraints governing retail land-use development parameters.

Private Owernship Key (**14**)
Darker Value = Most Private Space
Lighter Value = More Accessible Privately Owned Space

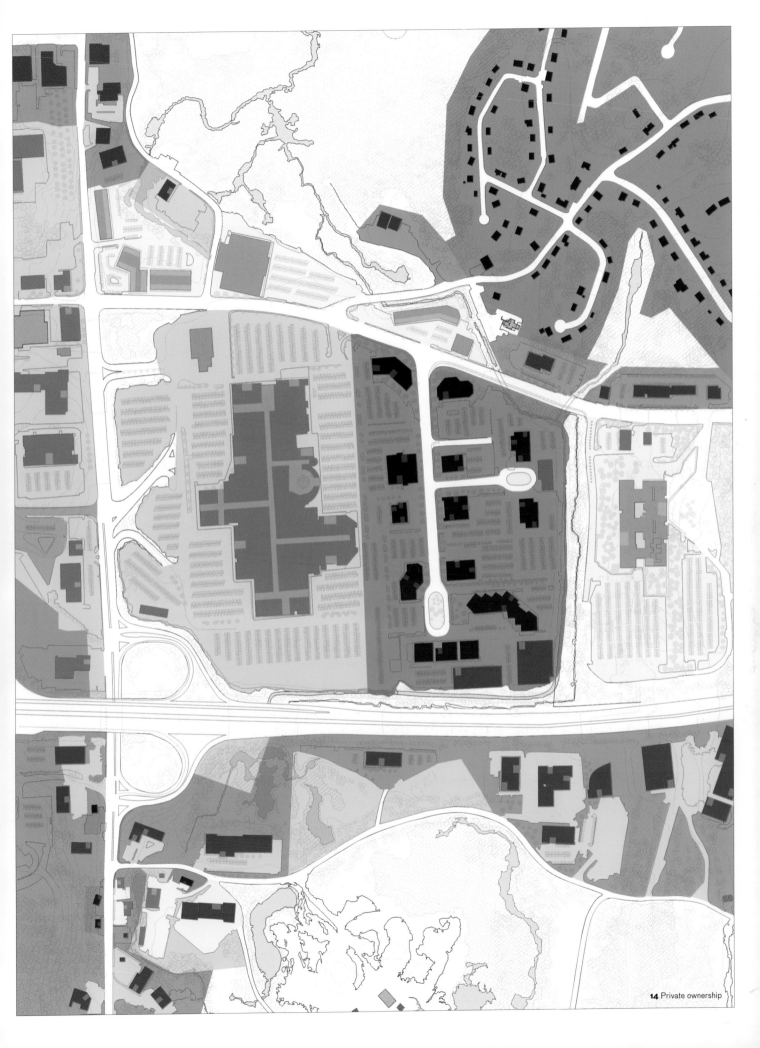

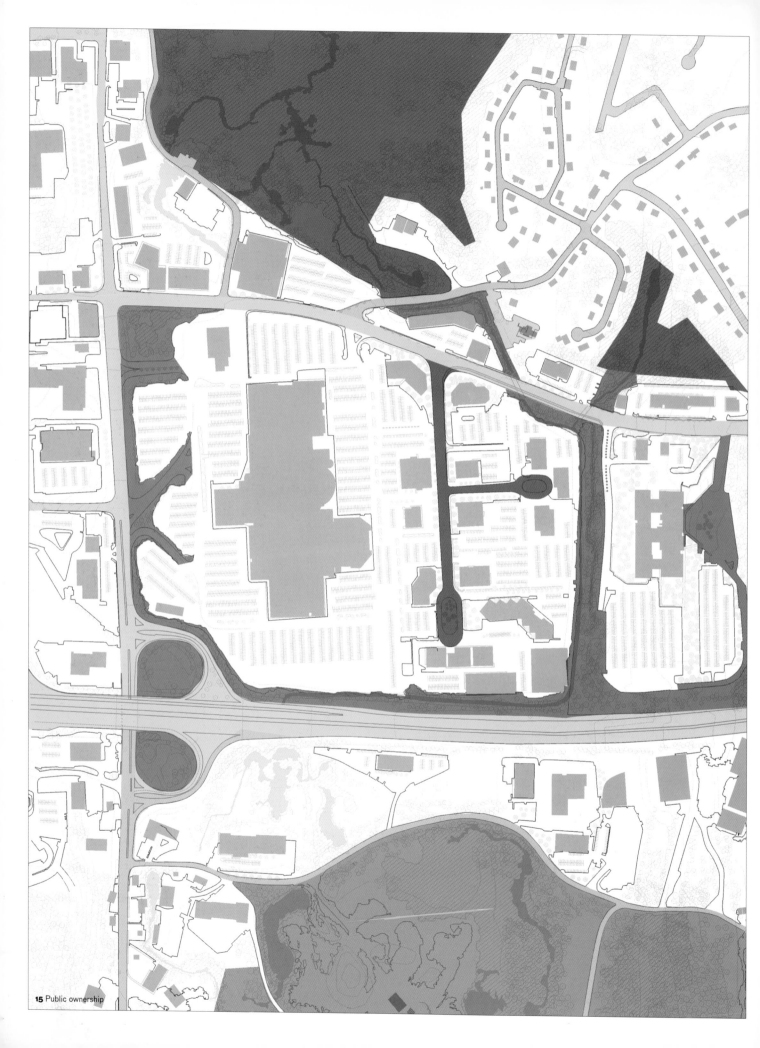

Private and Public Ownership

Most of the site is privately owned and controlled, with the exception of the conservation lands and roadways. Publicly controlled open space, where people can congregate without corporate defined constraints to their behavior, is nonexistent. The mall's central spine is truly public only in appearance, not in its civic role as a public forum protected by constitutional rights.

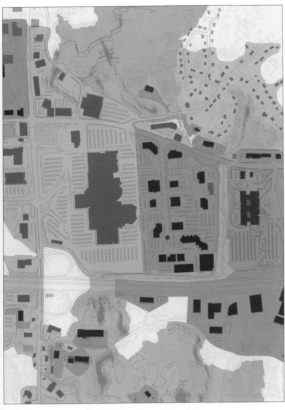

16 Zoning

Zoning

Zoning can be loosely defined as town regulations that set preferred land uses, densities, building heights, and other restrictive conveyances. Typical of suburban communities, single-use zoning is the norm. Burlington has for decades relied on discretionary zoning to gain negotiation power with developers. By mandating low FARs for parcels ripe for development, the town requires developers to apply for variances. In strong economic times the town can extract large subsidies from developers for pet projects like schools, infrastructure, and services, while poor economic climates result in developers extracting concessions from town officials. This has created an uneven and unpredictable playing field, one subject to the vagaries of the economy, and the personalities of the town elders.

Zoning

Retail and office uses dominate the site. Each zoning area is defined discretely (as a single use) from its neighboring districts. Uses do not overlap. The shapes of the districts are irregular and are the result of optimizing market forces, topography, ownership, negotiations between the city and landowners, and accidents of history.

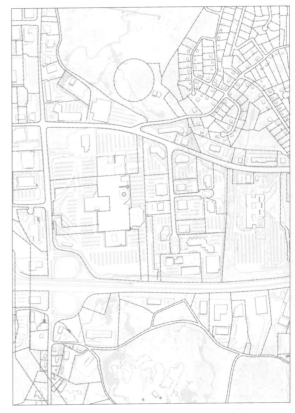

17 Property lines

Property Lines

Surprisingly, the largest parcel is not the mall, but the clinic. The mall and office sites are subdivided into smaller parcels to reflect the complex leasing and legal agreements between developers and tenants. For instance, anchor stores in the mall control their own property and parking lots, while the mall owner controls the atriums and parking spaces. This ownership model allows the individual anchors to retain greater legal, and financial, control while placing the economic burden for sustaining the infrastructure on the mall's owners.

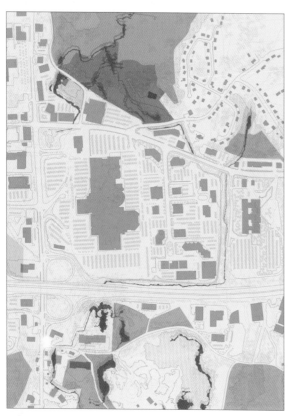

18 Conservation lands

Conservation Lands

Conservation lands are located on three parts of the site. These areas consist of a mix of woodlands and wetlands. The northern site, which is also part of the aquifer re-charge zone, is fenced off from public access to protect the water supply.

Programming

Programming examines how people use a space, and may or may not coincide with original zoning categories. Programming looks at hourly, daily, weekly, and seasonal patterns of use as well.

19 Programming: Morning, activity intensity

Morning

Workers arriving at work concentrate activity in and around offices, stores, and cafes. The mall has barely begun to prepare for the day. Lahey Clinic, always a hub of activity, begins visiting hours, operations, and doctor's visits.

Noon

Workers from neighboring offices, as well as neighboring communities, flock to the mall during lunchtime to run errands, shop, and eat at its expansive food court. Those seeking respite from sterile office environments populate the slivers of green open spaces.

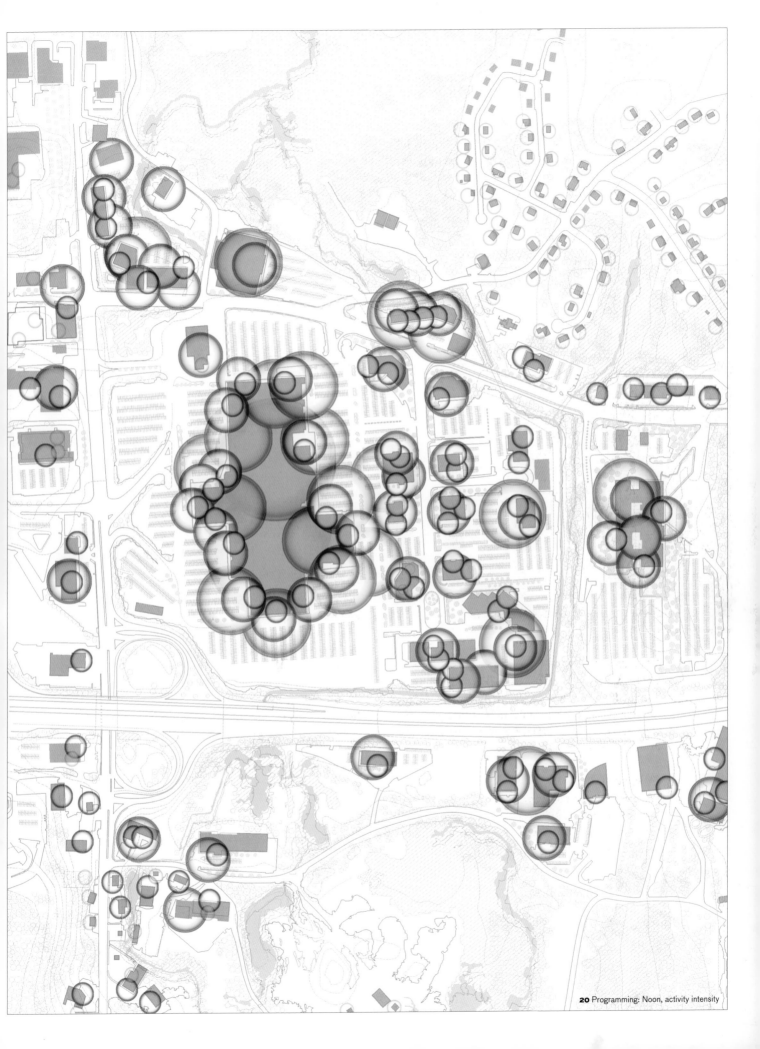

21 Programming: Evening

22 Figure-ground

Evening

Offices close for the day and Burlington becomes an entertainment and shopping mecca. Restaurants, movie theaters, bookstores, and churches become hubs of activity. The mall's parking lot is nearly always full from 6–9 p.m. The clinic is active with evening visitors and late night emergencies.

Buildings

Buildings take on a number of different forms and configurations, determined as much by program needs as building conventions, economic constraints, market forces, and cultural preferences.

Figure-Ground

The figure-ground analysis reveals a variety of building typologies, small and large, regular and irregular. There is only fragmentary evidence of a cohesive urban fabric and structure.

Structure

Structural system orientations vary from building to building and are influenced by parking.

Entries

Entrances are reciprocally linked to the size, location, and orientation of the parking fields. Only rarely do the entrances relate to one another (as in the office park).

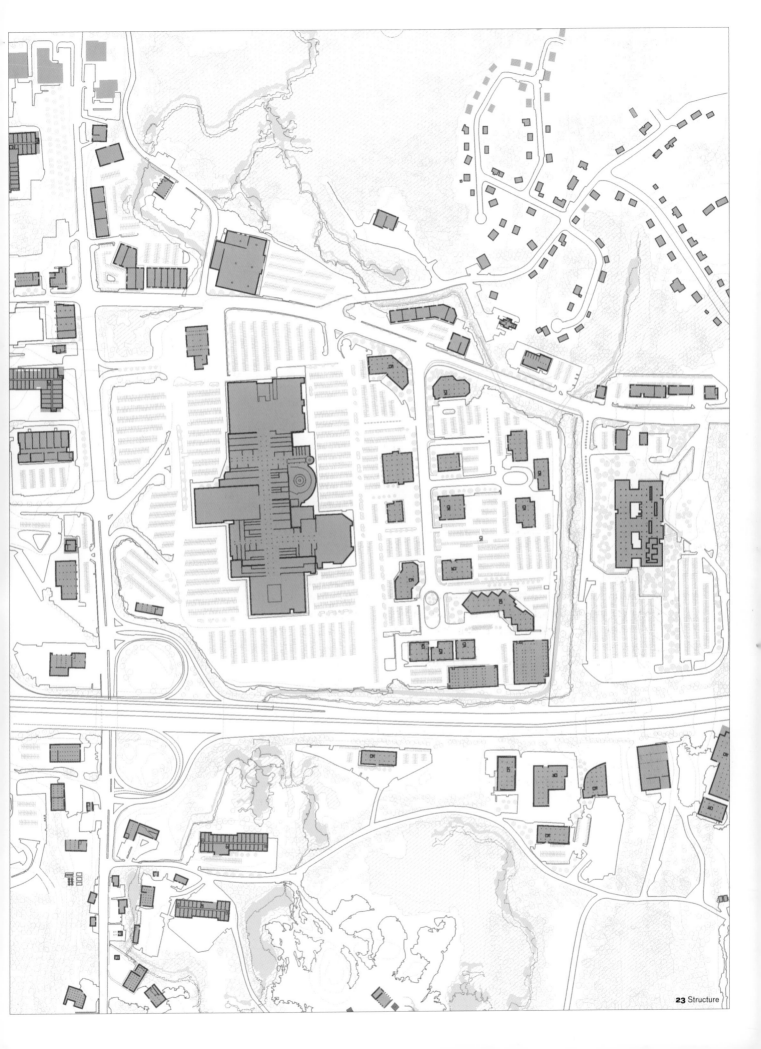

Landmarks

Landmarks are the means by which we orient ourselves in a context. The recognition of a landmark will depend on who perceives it and whether or not it is legible and distinguishable among a site's other prominent features. A landmark for a child might be a toy store, while a trucker may view a gas station or a rest stop as a significant marker. Size, height, use, location, and color are just some of the variables that determine landmarks.

25 Cultural landmarks

24 Visual landmarks

Visual Landmarks

Lahey Clinic sits atop a plateau like a Hellenistic acropolis. A fourteen-story office tower distinguishes itself from its three-story neighbors by virtue of height. The three slender radio transmission towers to the north of Mall Road are most obvious at night when their red lights flash, warning off planes from nearby Hanscom Airfield.

Cultural Landmarks

A church tucked behind the intersection of Mall Road and Lexington Road is located in close proximity to the historic sites of demolished parishes. A more prominent culture landmark is the Barnes and Noble bookstore on Middlesex Turnpike. This national chain has become a library, coffee house, salon, and general hangout for singles, couples, and literary types, especially on weekend evenings.

This in turn will affect the market value of a lease. Even within a mall, the relative value of each store varies significantly. Location, context, visibility and traffic are factors contributing to the perceived value of each parcel.

Another way of measuring value is through an analysis of assessed values assigned by a town or city, and its tax rate. Town governments periodically assess the value of all properties within their borders based on a relative scale often tied to (discounted) market rates. The cumulative value of all the properties multiplied by the tax rate needs to be sufficient to cover the cost of running the town government. A lower tax rate can indicate a better, more efficiently run town and the possibility of generating higher profit margins. It can also indicate a lower standard of services, infrastructure, schools, and other public amenities.

26 Corporate landmarks

Corporate Landmarks
Several corporate headquarters sit in close proximity to Route 128. The change in elevation (150 feet) allows the dramatic presentation of each building to eastbound highway traffic. Large and bold corporate logos adorn these rather simple structures on the south side of the highway.

Capital Flows
While land is, economically speaking, immobile, it serves as a vehicle for the dynamic flow of capital over time. Land values manifested through leasing rates and property values, which fluctuate over time are based on market perceptions, supply and demand, and their ability to generate revenue streams. Developing the land to its highest and best use maximizes revenues. For instance, high traffic commercial developments such as regional malls are considered better uses than light industrial space or warehouses, as malls will tend to generate more income. One way of valuing retail property is to measure its capacity for generating sales in "dollars/square feet."

27 Land values

Land Values
Land values tend to be highest for lots north of the highway and abutting major roads. Residential districts have

lower values. Localized variations exist and are based on ease of access and visibility from the road.

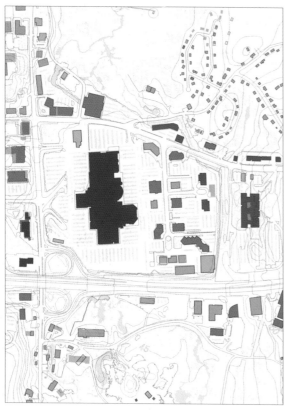

28 Building values

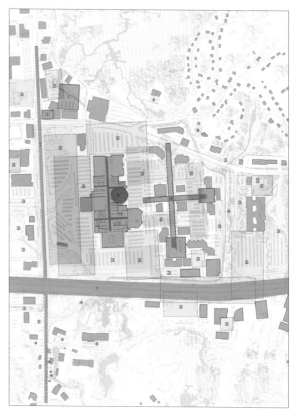

29 Figural spaces

Building Values

Building values are closely tied to land values. The mall, office complex, and clinic have the highest values, significantly higher than some of the smaller commercial buildings.

Sensory Readings

Our sensory experience of a place can be mapped. Subtle clues can be discerned from the often overwhelming abundance of sensory "noise" that bombards us whether we are driving down a strip or along a highway.

Figural Spaces

Some spaces can be described by a figure or shape. Analyzing figural spaces can help us understand relationships between objects and spaces. Is there a dominant shape? Are there specific types of relationships between spaces? Do they reveal underlying order or chaos? Despite its laissez-faire design and construction process, Burlington has some very well-defined figural spaces, bounded by buildings, vegetation, or changes in topography. However, the content of some grand spaces is banal: parking. Scale doesn't match significance. Furthermore, with the exception of the office complex, the order and relationship of spaces to one another is haphazard.

Sight Lines

In our visually oriented world, the role of signs, graphics, and symbols shapes our perception of the environment. Nevertheless, buildings, their shape, size and location, still play a significant role in forming our experiences. Mapping techniques, inspired by cinematographic

processes, can illustrate a series of spaces sequentially. Frames are linked to each other to depict movement. Drawings in two dimensions attempt to depict the four-dimensional experience of parallax.[1] The direction of travel (driving northeast vs. southwest) on Route 128 provides very different vantages and experiences of the mall and its environs.

Driving Southwest on Route 128

The elevated topography and trees shield views of Lahey Clinic and most of the office complex.

32 Southwest on Mall Road

Driving Southwest on Mall Road

The gently curving road, bounded by trees and loosely scattered buildings, creates a more bucolic setting, in contrast to the gritty landscape along the highway's edge.

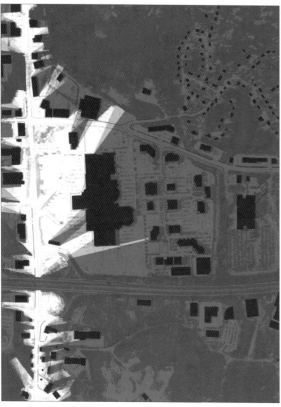

31 North on Middlesex

Driving North on Middlesex Turnpike

Buildings on the west of Middlesex Turnpike define a more continuous edge to the road, while the eastern edge is more open and exposed.

33 Southeast through the office complex

Driving Southeast through the Office Complex

The tree-lined boulevard and the alignment of the office buildings help form a continuously defined edge. The tower at the road's end terminates the view corridor, serving as a local and regional landmark.

Visual

Light has a profound effect on the way we perceive space. Slick office buildings create glare which presents a safety hazard to motorists, but also limits the visual information they can process. Similarly, rapidly alternating areas of light and shade make it difficult for the eye to adjust. Lighting levels can be measured (in lumens) and documented, thereby creating quantitative readings of perceptual phenomena. A deeper, perhaps painterly understanding of the quality of light particular to a specific site, its climate, and time of day is represented best through direct observation, photographs, and sketches.

34 Light levels (in lumens)

Light Levels

Light levels are greatest in open spaces, in particular in the parking lots. Vegetation and changes in topography significantly reduce glare.

Sound

As the blind can attest, sound reflects the shape and character of a space and the bodies that inhabit it. Standing at a crosswalk along a busy road, we are aware of cars and trucks, their proximity, relative speed, and direction without necessarily seeing them. A dense forest absorbs sound, but buildings, asphalt, and rock reflect it harshly.

Sound Levels

Decibel levels vary radically across the site. They are highest along the highway, Middlesex Turnpike, and parts of the mall's parking lot. But they can drop significantly when shielded by buildings or significant shifts in topography, even when standing close to the highway.

Olfactory

The early morning smells emanating from bakeries in narrow alleys are as integral to experiencing Paris as climbing the Eiffel Tower. The smell of suntan lotion on the beaches of Rio's Copacabana, chestnuts roasting in winter on New York's Park Avenue, fish being cleaned in a Japanese harbor, or fresh manure laid on the steep fields of alpine farms all provide strong olfactory signals to our brains which forever link smells with our associations of place. The recurrence of a smell can trigger distant memories. While no uniform means of measuring and documenting smells exists, observations can describe concentrations of different types of smells.

Olfactory Readings

It is no accident that Burger King spews out the smell of "charcoaled" beef toward Middlesex Turnpike. The smell of food (highlighted in yellow) creates strong attractors around the mall's food court. In other places the sweet smells of the forests and marshes temper vehicular fumes.

Endnotes

1   Parallax is the change in the arrangement of surfaces defining space due to the change in position of a viewer. See Steven Holl, *Parallax* (New York: Princeton Architectural Press, 2000), 26.

35 Sound readings (in decibels)

Olfactory Smells Key (**36**)
Yellow = Food
Orange = Active Exhaust
Sienna = Sedentary Exhaust
Ocher = Trees
Green = Fields
Blue = Wetlands
Light Blue = Water

36 Olfactory smells

Cross-Mapping

Cross-mapping illustrates the relationship between two or more systems, sets of attributes, or phenomena at a time. It is a very effective tool in identifying problems, challenges, and opportunities confronting a community. For instance in the Burlington case study, cross-maps of bus routes and sidewalks revealed very weak connections between both systems, indicating that navigating safe pedestrian routes for transit users around Burlington's Mall was difficult at best. Shedding light on this problem and its consequences (low ridership) also focuses attention on potential solutions, such as coordinating more effective bus routes, or expanding the network of sidewalks.

Cross-maps can also inform us about a site's underlying order, and the causal relationships between systems. For instance, the location of a major roadway in a city built on flat terrain will probably influence, even dictate, the location of buildings along that roadway, and not vice versa. Hierarchically speaking, the roadway is at a higher level than the buildings. On the other hand, a roadway's route in a hilly terrain is based in part on negotiating the terrain and potential obstacles. In this example, the roadway and its buildings are hierarchically at a lower level than the terrain. The terrain influences the location of the roadway which influences the location of the buildings.

However, there are many cases in contemporary cities where these conventional hierarchical orders are violated for economic, engineering, or historic reasons. For instance, it may be desirable and economically feasible for a roadway to cut through a mountainous terrain, or for a roadway's geometry to be adjusted to accommodate a large municipally scaled structure. In these cases, the hierarchical relationships change so that terrain does not always determine the location of roads and their buildings. The systems that generated a city mutate to accommodate changing needs. As cities grow and the needs of the populace become more complex, hierarchical patterns are altered, mutated, transgressed, and violated. A heightened awareness of these relationships allows for a more nuanced design response, capable of selectively negotiating and editing factors which contribute to a community's evolving identity.

A few examples of the many permutations of cross-maps available pertaining to Burlington follow.

1 Cross-mapping matrix

Topography + Infrastructure (Highway)

The original Route 128 was a two-lane road connecting town center to town center from Hingham to Salem. Expanding the road into a six-lane highway would have destroyed the towns it was meant to serve. Highway engineers needed a new path that skirted small villages as it circumscribed the greater Boston metropolitan area.

Upon cursory inspection of a regional map, Route 128 seems to follow a circular arc for much of its trajectory; closer examination reveals that the highway meanders slightly to the left and right of its idealized geometry. There are several reasons for this: one is to avoid existing buildings, landmarks, and obstructions; another is that a gradual grade can accommodate greater volumes of traffic at higher speeds. While engineers kept the highway to low and level elevations its path unavoidably intersected a hill in Burlington, leaving the engineers two choices. They could avoid the hill entirely by taking a wide sweeping curve around its base, or they could climb the hill at a reasonable slope. The engineers selected a path that traversed it just below its crest. In order to minimize the slope, the engineers cut into the hillside, requiring additional retaining walls on the highway's northern side. The dirt or "fill" generated by the cut, was used to create an embankment in the valley and its wetlands immediately west of the hilltop, thereby reducing the highway's slope when approaching the hill.

With the exception of the Romans, most preindustrial societies avoided earthmoving in order to accommodate roadways because the energy, resources, and know-how required were not available or viable. This cross-map shows how in Burlington, the natural hierarchical relationship (topography determining road) has been overridden because the resources and economics supported this option. This map also reveals the engineer's logic in determining the route, ratio of cut and fill, and highway's optimal slope.

2 Topogaphy

3 Infrastructure

Infrastructure (Highway) + Sensory Readings (Sound)

The highway is a major source of noise in Burlington. Noise levels differ across the site for a variety of reasons. First, the source of the sound must be considered. Is it a rumbling Harley-Davidson, or a silky quiet hybrid automobile? The aerodynamics of the vehicle, brand of tire, velocity, and acceleration all impact noise levels.

Secondly, changes in traffic volume can impact noise levels. As traffic slows during rush hour, noise levels reduce commensurately. Conversely, when traffic flows freely, noise levels increase, as the continuous stream of vehicles traveling at over seventy miles per hour stream by, punctuated by the sound of downshifting trucks on the hill, and vehicles accelerating while accessing on-ramps.

Thirdly, the location and distance of the sound source relative to where it is heard impacts how sound is perceived. The elevation profile of the highway alongside the Burlington Mall varies. At one point the highway is twenty feet above the mall's parking lot. While standing next to the highway at this point, the noise is hardly perceptible, as the noise travels 20 feet overhead. Sound generated at this height does not directly reach a person standing in the parking lot; instead, it travels overhead and bounces off distant objects, buildings, and is muffled and diffused before reaching a person's ears. A counter-example occurs where the highway cuts into the hill. The site's acoustics are amplified by a large embankment, where the noise bounces off retaining walls and rock outcroppings.

Decibel levels metered at regular intervals can be cross-mapped against infrastructure, topography, vegetation, and building footprints, to document how sound characteristics change along the highway, providing clues about why decibel levels vary, and what can be done to manage unwanted noise.

5 Infrastructure

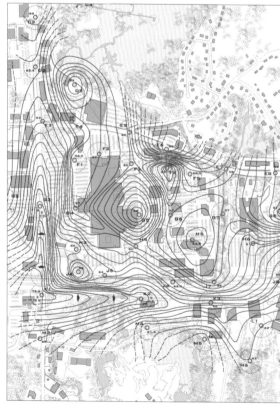

6 Sound

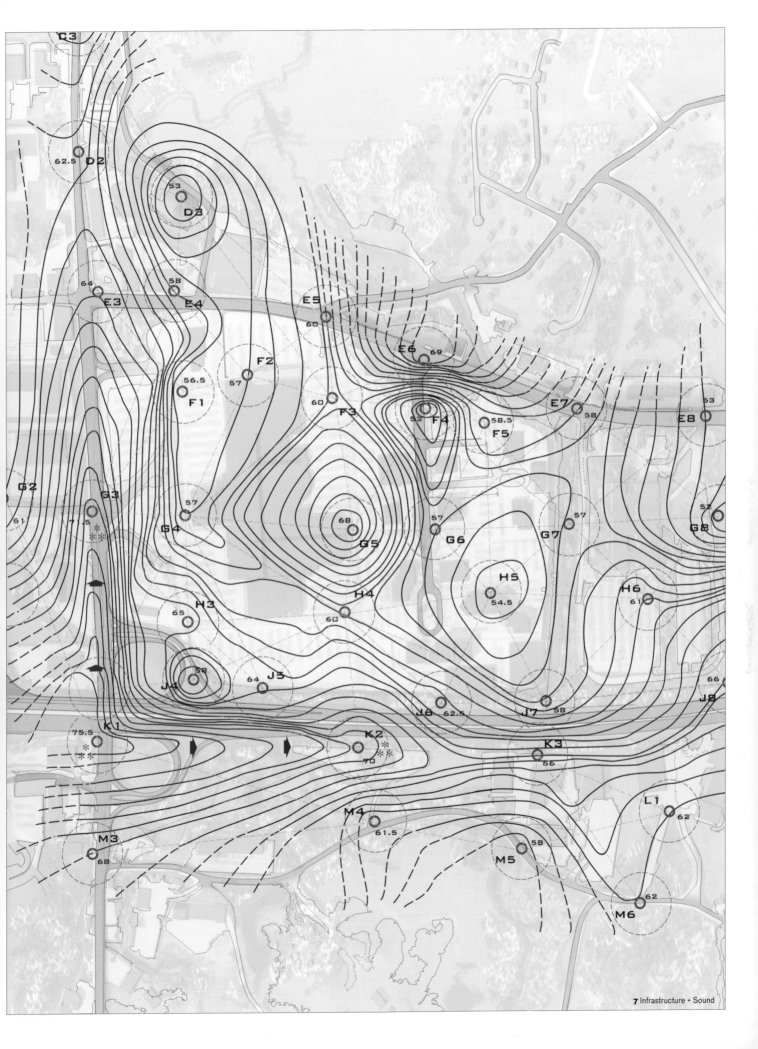

Sensory Readings (Sound) + Zoning

How do noise levels affect the types of uses that can be found along the highway versus areas set further back from the highway? Zoning immediately along the highway has changed since the '50s from largely light industrial uses (warehouses, manufacturing facilities, and gravel pits) to commercial, and institutional uses. Burlington's convenient location attracted growing companies that built inexpensive structures with large asphalt parking fields. The fact that some of these structures were relatively close to the highway and its noise did not matter to the original occupants who were more industrial than later tenants. Advances in building technologies (hermetically sealed buildings, nonoperable windows, air conditioning, and Muzak) helped create acoustically isolated buildings.

Overlaying these two maps illustrates a band of commercial, office, and institutional uses running parallel to the highway. It also shows how recently constructed office buildings and complexes (Sun Micro Systems and Oracle) are getting closer to the highway.

This trend can be attributed in part to the increased land values, creating economic incentives for developers to maximize their returns by building the largest building mass possible on a parcel. In addition, image conscious firms gain a stronger presence along the highway, by prominently positioning their structures and signage so that they are visible to thousands of motorists daily.

Conversely, other uses such as housing, recreation, schools, and retail, which support Burlington's populace, are zoned well back from the highway to provide some acoustic privacy.

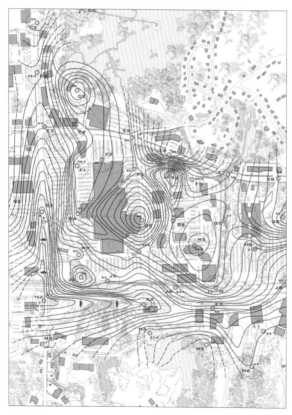

8 Sound

9 Zoning

Zoning + Buildings

Burlington's development patterns have been largely the
result of "discretionary zoning" policies exercised by
the town's planning department over the last fifty years.
Consequently, this process provides developers with a
great deal of leeway in negotiating on a parcel-by-parcel
basis, the size, program, and configuration of a project.
Historically, very few limits were placed on how the
parcels were reconfigured, or subdivided, allowing developers great freedom in assembling land tracts in ways
that suit their financial objectives. Developers were however required to meet certain parking-footprint ratios.
Cross-mapping zoning and buildings demonstrates how
each building type is plopped onto the site in seemingly
arbitrary configurations. Developers and their designers
molded the shape of their developments on generic office
and retail building types adjusted to work reciprocally
with more malleable parking fields. Little regard was
given to the consequences of this process or to Burlington's spatial order and landscape.

11 Zoning

12 Buildings

Buildings + Capital Flows

In rural settings, land can generate capital through farming, grazing, logging, mining, or drilling for oil. In more urban contexts, land generates value by virtue of the types of buildings that occupy the land. The highest and best use typically generates larger revenue streams. For instance, on a per-square-foot basis, the land beneath a one-story ranch house will be of less value than a similarly sized parcel supporting a six-story office building. Deciding on the appropriate type of economic development for each site depends on a number of factors. Those include a consideration of adjacent uses, competition, and the ability of a neighborhood to economically sustain desired uses. For example, a developer may wish to build an exclusive shopping center featuring high-end boutiques. If the demographic profile within a prescribed market area does not have the financial resources required to afford the shops, a lower-end shopping center may be more viable for this target audience. Because revenues and profits generated by a low-end retailer will be lower, leases and land values will also be reduced.

Over time however, land values can increase as retail volumes and revenues increase, which in turn attracts more development potential. Shops and surrounding sites upgrade their facilities, and land values rise accordingly.

This phenomenon has played itself out in Burlington since the mall was first built. The mall serves as a magnet for development, and the sites around it have been occupied by small and mid-sized retailers (like Barnes and Noble), chain restaurants, multiplex cinemas, hotels, and auto dealerships, all of whose business models depend in part on their proximity to the mall. Together, this amalgam of developments generates high traffic and revenue streams. If recent trends continue, it is likely that the mall will continue to grow in size and density, and secondary and tertiary business such as the auto dealership could be replaced by higher uses.

By overlaying the buildings (and a description of their uses, scale, and densities, etc.) with information about capital flows, it is possible to evaluate the relationship between these two site characteristics. The relationship can inform future development on the site.

14 Buildings

15 Capital Flows

Capital Flows + Ownership

The size and configuration of parcels can reveal important clues about ownership, potential uses, zoning constraints, and legal and financial factors. In addition, they can convey information about the historic interplay of these factors over time. Ownership is legally expressed through a deed, which describes the size and configuration of a parcel and the limits and easements placed on that parcel. The value of the parcel is a function of its location, size, ease of access, and adjacent uses among other factors. In Burlington, location of the parcels, and size of the parcels are primary factors in determining the value of the properties and the flow of capital they support as measured by tax assessors' maps.

With few exceptions, large institutions, corporations, and developers control the strategic parcels along the highway, Middlesex Turnpike, and Mall Road. Parcel size in this area tends to be large, meeting the needs of the owners and their building types. The mall's land, for instance, is made up of five large parcels: one for each of the three anchor tenants and two for the mall's owner (one for the central atrium spine, the other for the parking fields). This condition reflects the unique financial and legal definitions between mall operators and their principal anchor tenants. In contrast, suburban residential tract housing is more straight forward, where swaths of residential development north of Mall Road are comprised of small parcels (1/8–1/2 an acre) owned primarily by middle-class homeowners. Individual building footprints are small (1,000–2,000 square feet). The geometry of tract housing developments is malleable, and can be clustered in a variety of configurations, allowing the negotiation of rolling terrain north of Mall Road. This land's potential for generating greater value is limited though, given that it may be harder to assemble large tracts of land, and convert them to higher yielding commercial or institutional uses.

Certain areas are undervalued, in particular at the intersection of Middlesex Turnpike and Mall Road, where mid-sized parcels dominate. Given the site's visibility, future development opportunities exist for the clever developer, who can realize its economic potential.

17 Capital Flows

18 Ownership

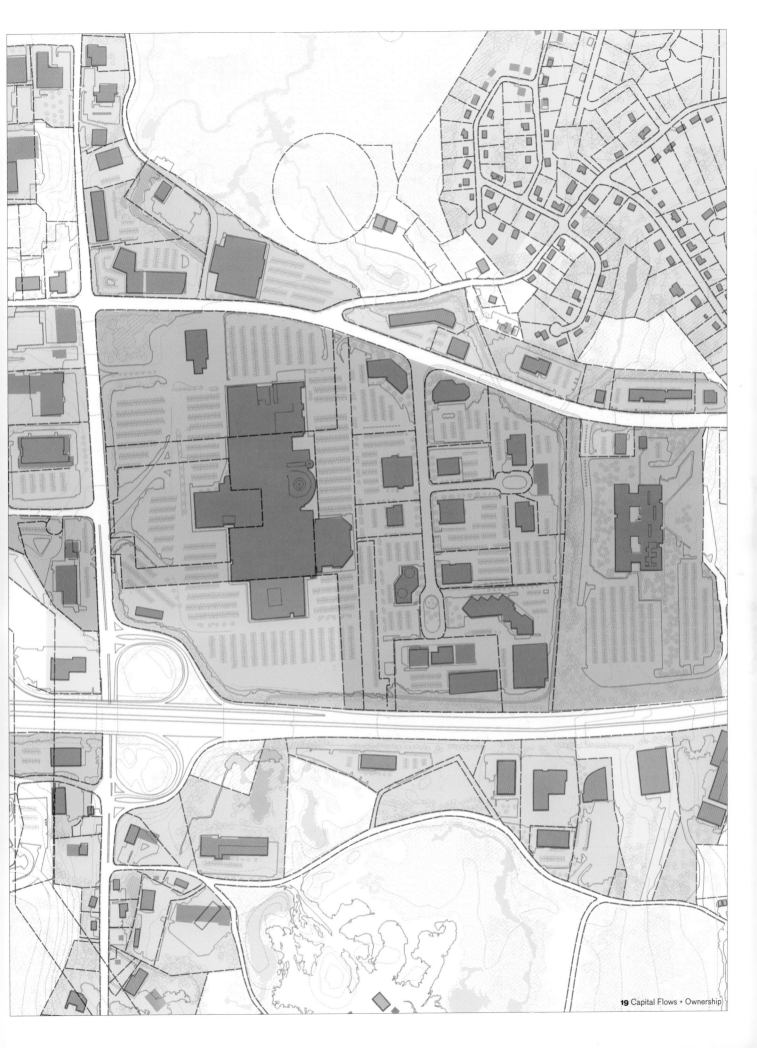

Editing

The mapping process generates facts, information, and documented phenomena of a site. Editing involves uncovering a site's useful history, engaging that history, evaluating site forces, and assessing the community's values. This is where a vision for transformation begins, by deciding what information to use, and what sets of values and processes filter this information for future design purposes.

Distilling Useful History

As we have seen from the proposition "Identity = Site + Time," when "time" or history is erased, the identity of a site is temporally shallow, and therefore lacks identity. Historic preservationists have provided worthwhile tools for sustaining valuable historic structures and districts. But history is living and dynamic, reflecting powerful societal forces, which in turn help shape our environment's identity.

To uncover a site's history, the first decision a community needs to consider is what to erase, what to maintain, and what to build upon through transformation. Considering the useful history of any element or system in the environment is helpful in arriving at a decision. Can a historic element find a purpose through its reuse or its transformation, now, or in the near future? Defining useful purposes is subjective, of course, and will reflect a community's predilections. Use need not be utilitarian; it can be symbolic or cultural. A valued use may also be latent, absent today but available for future engagement. Conservation lands can, for instance, fulfill this role, as can seasonal structures and performance pavilions. Determining a time threshold before realizing delayed utility is affected by economic as well as community criteria.

Engage a Site's History

However legible, every site has a history, be it geological, environmental, or man-made. Man-made site histories often result from the intervention of multiple parties motivated by a wide range of factors and their actions exercised on a site, over time. These actions are often recorded in the physical terrain of our environment. They contribute in creating identity. The more temporally layered and idiosyncratic the interplay between a community and its people over time, the more one place will differentiate itself from another. To erase all vestiges and traces of past interventions is to lose any reference to time, thereby temporally isolating and encapsulating proposed developments from past interventions. Engaging a site's useful history can be achieved by carefully reading, writing, and tracing site conditions, but never erasing everything.

For instance in Burlington, engaging a site's recent history can be exercised through the transformation of the mall, a significant structure in the region, not only in scale, but in its economic, social, and cultural role. While the mall's steel structure is easily adapted to many uses (office, housing, or recreation), its spine might be transformed into a new kind of public space, where people meet and congregate, but not necessarily under the gaze of a mall's security staff.

The mall helped make Burlington a destination, and its grandly scaled public spine can be transformed to support an identity tied to traces of its past, however recent.

Similarly, infrastructure has played an important historical roll in Burlington's history. Since the first inns were built along the Middlesex Turnpike in the early 1800s, Burlington has been an important crossroads. The mapping process has revealed to us the reciprocal relationship between topography and infrastructure in Burlington's landscape. The engagement of the site's rich history could be enhanced through the coordinated and integrated transformation of the landscape abutting the highway that currently scars this place, thereby creating a new expression of man and nature linked by memory.

It is essential, before commencing design and development, to map and read a site thoroughly and to be fully aware of the sometimes hidden richness embedded there. The designer then has the option to selectively ignore or engage its history, by building upon it, or building relative to traces of its history.

Evaluate Forces at Work

All parties engaged in the Adaptive Design Process not only need to consider historic forces operating on a site, but contemporary ones as well. Capital flows, power reflected through ownership, the role of infrastructure, zoning and land-use patterns, environmental factors, and other social conditions are but a few of the forces that play themselves out on a site and need to be evaluated and engaged as part of any transformation proposal.

Ignoring contemporary site forces will yield designs which are disconnected temporarily from the here and now.

Community Values

Implicitly, the editing process is value laden. Ultimately, decisions about editing will reflect the values of a community, or client group. But the designers and analysts assisting communities carry their own biases. These biases are active when filtering vast amounts of information created by the mapping process, and consequently will influence the design proposals. For this reason, it is important to be explicit about the values held by all parties engaged in the Adaptive Design Process. To that end, the author is sharing his values below, as a means of shedding light on factors that influence the case studies, and which could be employed to create identity in any community.

With Increased Density, Add Landscape (Natural and Artificial)

Continued increases in urban growth and density are inevitable as human settlement patterns continue to try to accommodate the needs of a rapidly growing populace. This populace in turn needs to be sustained by an increasingly complex and expansive system of services and infrastructure. This need for expanded space and service has been accommodated in urban areas by increasing the capacity of existing urban systems and making existing cities denser, or by claiming more space beyond the limits of existing city boundaries, fostering low-density sprawl. Further complicating this dynamic is the American desire of individuals to claim their own territory and dwell in free-standing structures, free of bounded adjacencies, and connected to open landscapes. With the ubiquitous export of American popular culture and values, the American Dream finds itself easily transplanted from Silicon Valley to the Yangtze River in China. Paradoxically, this desire to claim some portion of the landscape for one's own destroys that very landscape.

This design value acknowledges that growth is inevitable, while supporting the concept that higher densities have the ability to create more vibrant and dynamic "places" in the suburb if configured and clustered around preexisting metropolitan concentrations. It also recognizes that people have an innate desire to be close to landscape. These two seemingly contradictory objectives can be reconciled by resolving to add landscape as one increases a site's density. Where landscape has been destroyed or obliterated, the landscape can be revived or reconstructed. With technological advances, an "artificial landscape" or a newly constituted landscape can be created that balances the needs of a technologically advanced society with the need for landscape.

Connectivity: No Man or Building Is an Island

Most contemporary suburban commercial centers and strips are conceived of and built as a collection of autonomous buildings, or complexes having little if anything to do with adjacent buildings, sites or districts. This holds true not only for the buildings but the spaces they create and the infrastructure that supports them. Furthermore, the current design, development, and approval process that generates these environments is not concerned with creating continuities or connections between adjacent sites and their buildings, either in terms of their shapes and forms, or the materials, scale or use of the structures. This current process often yields a wide range of built structures and spaces of differing scales, materials, and uses, thrown together in ad hoc fashion to create a disconnected environment.

The "connectivity" between the elements that comprise a neighborhood/district, can be enhanced by developing each element (a building, complex, or space) as part of a larger integrated constellation of forms and spaces. This requires that each element have a high "valence" capacity, that is, it has the potential to couple or join with other elements. This can be achieved in part by sharing direct physical connections to streets, paths, and spaces. Greater continuities can also be achieved through association, by creating buildings and spaces that share common materials, scales, architectural elements (window size, structure, etc.), and orientation. The higher the valence capacity of an element, the greater the chance it has of contributing to a highly integrated network of streets, paths, space, buildings, and complexes capable of supporting a richer environment.

Open Space vs. Public Space: Defining the Shapes of Spaces

The current suburban condition often lacks well-defined spaces capable of supporting and sustaining public life.

As noted in "Connectivity," this is due in part to the development process, which creates autonomous and self-contained objects, spatially isolated from neighboring buildings and sites. It is very difficult for boxes or solitary objects to, on their own, create bounded space. By definition, at least two objects—with deliberate and calibrated relationships to one another—are required to create a space.

A public exterior place as a container for communal activities and life can be enriched by its direct adjacency to interior publicly oriented uses. Buildings brimming with life and activity should frame this space. These activities can spill out into public space, creating a vibrant and vital environment where the community can gather. Successful open public spaces are well defined both in plan and section. Open public space should have a sufficient amount of valence to couple and bond with other spaces and buildings.

Create Systems of Orientation/Landmarks

While the suburbs were created both by and for the automobile, poorly designed highways and their adjacent structures have created spaces that are disorienting to motorists and pedestrians alike. We have become desensitized to the degree of disorder in our visual environment and are often forced to navigate by trial and error, and eventually, by habit. The logic of highway intersections is driven more by the conventions of traffic engineering and the expediency of developers than careful consideration of way-finding through graphics and locations of building landmarks.

How then does one begin to create a more clearly integrated system of roads, paths, signs, and selective landmarks such that motorists and pedestrians can comfortably navigate this suburban landscape? By creating a system of landmarks integrated with a network of paths and roadways by which residents can orient themselves. Complimentary and coordinated systems of landmarks and networks could operate and overlap on all scales (regional, community, building complex, building, and room) so as to allow for easy transitions between variously scaled networks. For instance, if traveling on a highway, one might orient oneself relative to a system of vertical markers (or inhabited structures) which are similar in type, materials, scale, or lighting at key off-ramps. Their consistent spatial and typological relationships assist in providing a cognitive structure to the environment. Like a New England town punctuated by church steeples, important buildings and spaces are codified in the town's structure and also serve as a means of orienting oneself relative to the landscape and townscape.

Cruising: Integrate Pedestrian and Automobile Traffic

The automobile—or a reincarnation of another mode of transportation maximizing mobility and personal freedom—must be considered as an integral component of any new form of suburban development. The United States's geography, land-use patterns, and demographics are structurally ingrained, such that ignoring personalized mobility systems must be considered and tapped into as a source of active street life, especially in parallel with the pedestrian network. So many examples exist worldwide (Champs Elysées, Paris; Park Avenue, New York; Newbury Street, Boston) where the car and pedestrian coexist and in fact create a more dynamic and vibrant streetscape. Why not acknowledge the potential of the car to contribute to the life of suburban communities by taming its negative attributes—speed, mass, and smell—within newly configured networks of roads and walkways?

Selecting Tools: (Hybrid) Building Typologies and Design Tools

Utilizing existing as well as new design tools and strategies can assist in the creation of an environment possessing a strong sense of identity. What follows is a catalog of tools and strategies that touch upon issues associated with infrastructure, programming, land-use, suburban fabric, building types, hybrid landscape typologies, green buildings, and taming parking.

New Infrastructure Typologies

Because suburbia found its genesis in the rapid development of highways in the 1950s, a reevaluation of highway design conventions is long overdue. Highway design standards that maximize efficiency and safety often consume excessive acres of landscape and townscape without a balanced regard to impact on preexisting conditions. The design process employed by Christian Menn, a structural engineer from Switzerland, to develop the Leonard P. Zakim Bunker Hill suspension bridge (part of Boston's massive Central Artery Project) demonstrates that a balanced and thoughtful critique of design parameters driving conventional highway design and construction can lead to more compact and elegant design solutions for funneling traffic flows through dense environments.

development patterns. Instead of a conglomeration of randomly placed buildings, parking lots, signs, and other visual clutter, the highway can string along coherent patterns of urban form. These patterns, running primarily parallel to the highway, can support a wide array of uses, and feed off the energy of the highway, animating its edges by virtue of adjacency and transparency. Intensifying the development of urban form and density along the highway also frees up valuable terrain behind such developments and shields this terrain from unwanted highway noise.

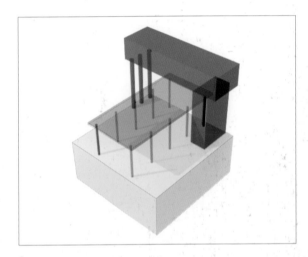

2

Creating Connections: Bridging over Infrastructure to Create Connections

Where highways or other forms of infrastructure sever urban development, it is possible to reconnect developments by bridging over infrastructure.[1] Footbridges, parking garages, train stations, and shopping malls could all be built over infrastructure.

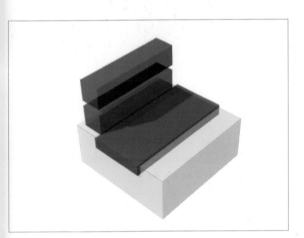

1

Infrastructure as an Armature: Building Parallel to Existing Infrastructure

Besides reconsidering the axioms of highway design—such as ramp design radii—shapes, frequencies, etc.—designers, developers, and planners need to consider the highway as an integral component of future

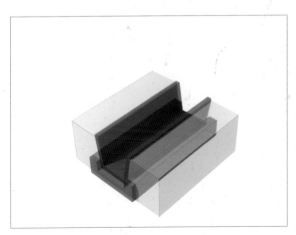

3

Creating Connections: Excavating under Infrastructure to Create Connections

Where building over roadways is impractical or prohibitive, blocks, districts, and regions can be linked through excavation. A city such as Montreal, where harsh winters would otherwise discourage pedestrian traffic, provides an extensive network of generously proportioned passageways and plazas, animated by retail and entertainment establishments. This network is integrated with the city's block structure to create a vibrant and active central business district. Subways and airports serve as models for creating vital and vibrant urban nodes by excavating beneath or building over existing infrastructure or natural impediments.

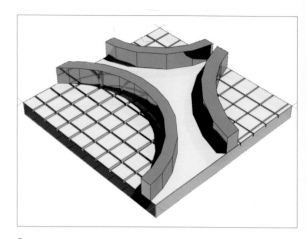

5

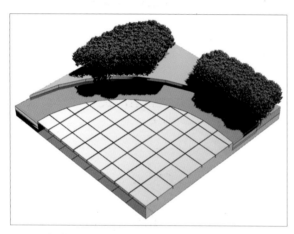

4

Infrastructure as a Buffer

In some conditions where highways cut through the landscape, the land and its vegetation can serve as a distinct zone of nondevelopable land. Examples include the idealized man-made representations of nature presented to urban motorists along the Saw Mill Parkway north of New York City, Olmsted's Emerald Necklace in Boston, or Lady Bird Johnson's Highway Beautification Program in Texas. It is also possible to create an art inspired intervention, such as artists Mags Harries and Lajos Héder's installations in Phoenix, where giant vessels and walls serve as sound abatement for neighborhoods abutting the highway.

Infrastructure as Container

Medieval Europe's defensive walls protected towns from invaders. They also helped define boundaries between urbanized areas and outlying farms and woodlands. As the need for city defenses declined, many of these historical walls were removed or transformed to serve contemporary purposes. Vienna converted its walls and glaciers into the elegant Ringstrasse, while some of Paris's walls have been transformed into new parkways. These vacated barriers can also be inhabited by highways or rail lines, encircling cities as a beltway. These transportation corridors can serve as armatures for feeding the growth of a city's girth, or as a protective boundary defining an edge between urban and rural areas.

Programming and Land-Use Strategies

One of the major contributing factors to the banal quality of most suburban contexts is the poor distribution and location of structures relative to one another in the landscape. A lively sense of community arises out of clusters of buildings, and the experiences they support, as well as the network of adjacent public spaces. The design of suburbs could be greatly improved through the thoughtful rearrangement of the buildings that are already in place. As buildings outlive their useful lifecycles, opportunities arise to remove, rebuild, or renovate each piece in the suburban landscape.

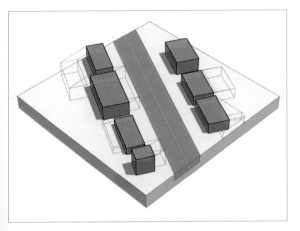

6

Redistribution of Building Mass (Reciprocity)

As the graphic analysis of Burlington illustrates, one of the major problems contributing to its functional inadequacies and visual incoherence is not so much the lack of dense development, but the poorly coordinated location of buildings relative to one another. As building lifecycles expire and structures need to be rebuilt, the redistribution over time of buildings, parking lots, and roadways, can incrementally generate more attractive, efficient, and coherent land-use patterns. Cities, like Las Vegas, are undergoing continuous and rapid transformations in response to economic forces and accelerated building lifecycles. The redistribution of land uses and building massing is evident on the strip. Where casinos once were set back from the strip, they now abut the road, as the scarcity of land dictates denser development and intensifies the need to promote each casino's visibility along the strip.

Intensification of Activity (Without Increasing Density)

Contemporary retail developers are masters in creating the appearance of intense areas of activity. The "Festival Marketplaces" developed in the 1970s and 1980s by James Rouse and Co. are excellent examples of a developer taking existing, often underutilized urban sites and infusing them with new life. By strategically concentrating retail and other public amenities along existing edges and nodes, urban life is concentrated and effective in creating lively environments. Increasingly, baseball parks, museums, and even airports are also becoming intense nodes infused with program and activity, encouraging both consumption and convivial interactions amongst patrons.

Virtually all of these precedents rely on enticing people to travel into zones of urban intensity. This added intensity increases demands on local and remote infrastructure. Combining housing with commercial and institutional developments could achieve the same results without added demands on infrastructure.

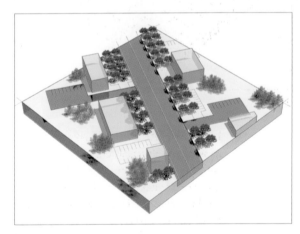

8

Reestablishing the Landscape Presence

Reestablishing the presence of landscape may be desired where residents of suburban communities seek a reprieve from asphalt. Suburban commercial strip developments and their adjacent sites may still have vestiges of a site's original landscape. The presence of the landscape can be strengthened by consolidating existing patches of green into legible and useful spaces, and,

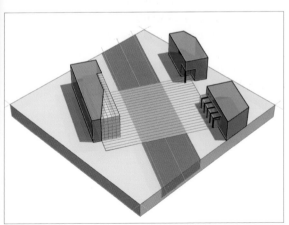

7

where possible, linking them with pedestrian paths. Where vital ecosystems have been compromised, it may be necessary to restore the landscape. Where equal demand exists for increased development and natural amenities, landscape can be built artificially on a newly constructed elevated platform, capable of sustaining urban and economically generated activities while maintaining the presence of the landscape.

Creating a Suburban Fabric

The morphology of the suburban condition is often deficient in two ways. First, it lacks identifiable urban places, places with figural spaces capable of supporting social interaction and public life not entirely based on consumption. Second, the suburb's current fabric—its organization of building types, open spaces, and street networks—often lacks a consistent or coherent structure. It is essential to establish a public realm and to link buildings and spaces together, creating a new suburban fabric. This is a point well defined and supported by the New Urbanists.

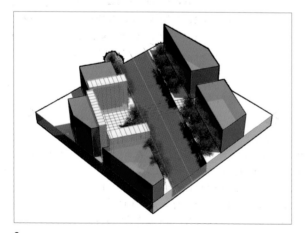

9

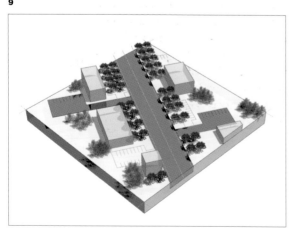

10

Creating New Public Spaces

Maximizing retailers and developers profits is a primary factor in determining the shape and location of public spaces in the suburbs. To foster true community interaction, clearly defined public plazas and spaces, interior and exterior, must be provided. The physical definition of such spaces can be achieved in part by adding buildings, structures, or landscape features to existing buildings, or by eliminating and carving out spaces from larger building volumes. This concept holds true for all scales and types of construction, whether it is a strip mall, an office park, or a mega-mall.

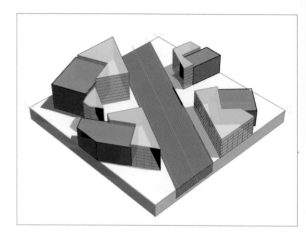

11

Creating and Morphing New Suburban Blocks

Many "livable" cities (Paris, London, Boston, Amsterdam, Kyoto, etc.) have balanced relationships between the number, size, and distribution of monuments (churches, institutions, and other distinct structures) versus buildings which serve as background fabric (housing, office space, and retail buildings.) The architecture of background structures are not necessarily monumental in scale or distinctive and do not distract from the more singular institutions and spaces of a city.

In the suburbs, new buildings are often designed to distinguish themselves from their neighbors despite serving the same mundane uses of housing, office space, and retail. What results is a visual cacophony of undistinguished buildings. New blocks could be created by adding new structures between existing structures, providing stronger visual and spatial continuity between buildings and spaces and their blocks.

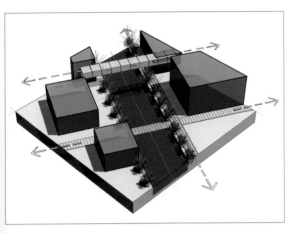

12

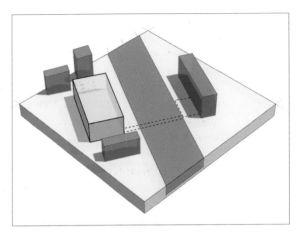

13

Stitching Connections between Places and Districts

The suburb's development process, characterized by parcel-by-parcel autonomous structures, creates, what Andres Duany refers to as contiguous sites, where "nearby is so far away."[2] Retail space could be right next to office space but be inaccessible because fences or roads impede access between adjacent sites. Large malls, offices, and apartments surrounded by parking lots rarely offer easy pedestrian, bicycle, or vehicular connections. The challenge of traversing sites located across major thoroughfares is even more perplexing and left only to the brave or foolhardy pedestrian.

By "stitching" connections through a network of pathways, bike paths, light rail, and other means of transit, mobility options are enhanced. This can also contribute to increasing the efficiency of delivering goods and services, and reducing automobile reliance. It will also create the kinds of connections that foster a sense of community.

New Building Types

Just as the elevator radically transformed the skyline of Chicago, new technologies will transform societies and their buildings.[3] William Mitchell describes how emerging digital technologies offer individuals, businesses, and institutions a wide array of possibilities for working together without geographical barriers.[4] The very definition of our homes, and the activities they support will change over time. Digital technologies will allow new urban structures to evolve, characterized by flexible relationships between producers, suppliers, distribution networks, and markets.

E-Building Types

Major on-line retailers like Amazon have allowed consumers to purchase a full range of products, delivered within twenty-four hours courtesy of FedEx. The frictionless economy allows for more direct, immediate distribution of goods and services, with fewer intermediate distributors and sales and marketing entities. Hypothetically, the cost of delivering goods should be cheaper, as distributors carry a lower overhead, and the expense of maintaining showrooms and retail staff is minimized if not eliminated. Inventory and financing costs are greatly reduced because retailers are more keenly attuned to the demands of the marketplace and adjust their production and warehouse capacity more quickly. Firms like Dell Computer deliver customized products with minimal inventory by commencing production of their products only once the purchaser has placed an order. Some e-tailers are developing small but strategically located showrooms that allow their client base to see their products in person. This model suggests that an entirely new building type, a cross between a warehouse and showroom, capable of supporting both conventional "shoppers" and "e-consumers" could evolve. The transformation of the marketplace typology from Rome's Trajan's Market, Istanbul's Great Bazaar, Paris's Bon Marché, to Minnesota's Mall of America is one that will continue to evolve as distribution networks and consumer needs change.

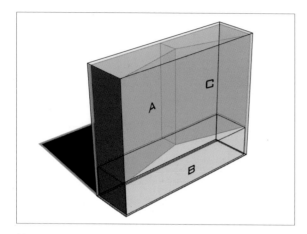

14

Time-Shared Uses

Time-sharing strategies can be useful when different uses can share the same space at different times in order to offset high rents or real estate costs. For instance, in Burlington, businesses with out-of-phase daily schedules (retail vs. office) have agreed to share parking lots. Similarly, in New York City, the city government has piloted programs that combine traditional school buildings during the daytime, with training and recreation services taking place in the evenings. Instead of valuable space (class rooms, gymnasiums, theaters, etc.) being left underutilized for long periods of time during the day or summer, these spaces can support the needs of a larger community throughout the day and seasons. The costs of operating the buildings and programs is greatly reduced and an active community center is created.

Infill Building Types (Malleable Building Types)

Burlington's figure ground analysis illustrates how the "fabric" of this district is comprised primarily of singular object-like buildings with little or no reference to one another. If a more cohesive "fabric" is to be achieved, and the existing structures are to remain, it will be necessary to develop and construct new buildings between existing structures. Such structures are often referred to as "infill" and are most commonly built in urban centers. Like a smile with a missing tooth, a new building fills the gap to create a continuous street edge.

Boston's Back Bay is an excellent example of how a limited number of 4–5 story townhouse buildings of uniform width (25 ft.) can create an environment that is visually ordered enough to create a harmonious neighborhood, while varied enough in its execution and detailing to create a lively street life. The challenge in the suburbs will be to develop a range of building types that are similar enough in size, structure, and materials that they can create visual continuity—through repetition—and harmony, and reconcile the numerous conflicting design conditions that exist in the suburbs between object-like structures.

New (Hybrid) Landscape Typologies

Is there a way to reconcile the seemingly contradictory needs of nature and suburban sprawl? The following strategies and typologies put forth tools that can help incorporate nature into the suburban domain.

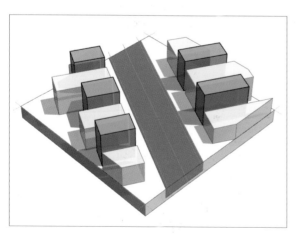

15

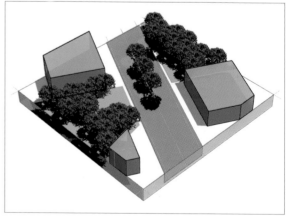

16

Rebuilding the "Lost Landscape"

Rebuilding a lost landscape involves restoring natural function and habitat to an area previously developed or degraded. Restoring some parcels may be economically challenging, unless combined with other project or infrastructure investments. Ecologists, landscape architects, and civil engineers can assist in achieving important goals such as providing storm filtering, flood control, and wildlife protection. Sports fields and other recreational areas may serve little ecological function, but provide human benefits such as encouraging good health and a stronger sense of community.[5]

The Burlington Mall's expansive parking structure was built above an aquifer. This unfortunate decision has had serious consequences for the landscape and community. The parking lot sinks, requiring filling and repaving every couple of years, and oil and other hazardous chemicals seep into the aquifer, endangering the town's water supply. Erasing the parking lot and rewriting the former landscape could protect the water supply and allow the aquifer to replenish itself.

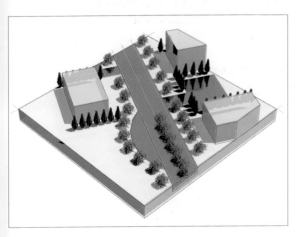

17

Constructing a "New Landscape"

The "New Landscape" attempts to remedy the scars of past human interventions through the design of parks and other man-made environments. These gardens and landscapes can provide vast improvements over impervious grayscapes, both ecologically and visually.

18

Harnessing Entropy: Edge City as Inhabited Ruin

As demonstrated by the inhabitation of ancient ruins in Rome, or abandoned steel mills in Germany's Ruhr Valley, opportunities for future redevelopment can be harnessed from the entropic forces acting on the built environment. Deliberate strategies to engage the forces of entropy allow nature to take over limited and selected portions of a site so that it might return back to nature as a ruin. In addition, selective erasure can accelerate a site's decay where desired.

For instance, large parking fields could be plowed and tilled, converting them to farms. Similarly, the selective destruction of a larger building or form, like the central spine of a mall, would allow a void to be converted to a winter garden. In turn this new "inhabited ruin" could serve as the organizing element around which future additions and transformations might occur.

19

Building an "Artificial Landscape": Landscape as Infrastructure

The artificial landscape can take on the role of infrastructure since it can support and sustain other uses. An artificial landscape creates a new, sometimes, elevated landscape above roads, highways, or rail lines, or on top of or over buildings. It helps provide additional space, light, and greenery around which other uses can be clustered and organized.

21

Green Roofscapes

Roofscapes can be considered an extension of the landscape. Replacing the largely unattractive roofscapes with vegetation and greenery can help achieve many benefits. Besides helping to mitigate the heat-island effect, green rooftops provide additional oxygen to the atmosphere and absorb storm water runoff. They can even provide a habitat for wildlife, as well as serve as public open space for a building's occupants. The Ford Factory designed by William McDonough is an enormous industrial complex with an expansive green roof. The additional cost of constructing this new landscape is more than offset by the lifecycle benefits in reduced energy costs.

While important structural and waterproofing issues need to be considered, green roofs are becoming increasingly viable.

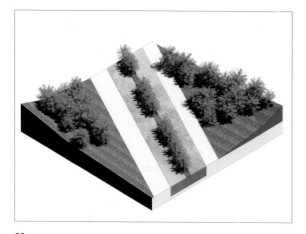

20

Divide and Conquer

Multilane feeder roads make pedestrian passage a life-endangering experience. Their enormous scale creates physical and visual barriers. Dividing traffic lanes can tame the scale of roadways and provide picturesque streets such as the tree-bounded *grande avenues* of Paris.

Ubiquitous Green Buildings

Why do edge cities have to be so gray? Why not green? This section suggests strategies for increasing the presence of landscape by establishing a variety of different vegetation types on, over, and within existing or new structures.

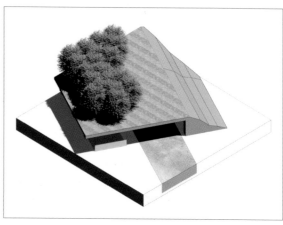

22

Green over Buildings

Instead of creating a green landscape, building by building, it is possible to build a new artificial landscape over existing or new structures. This can be accomplished by building a large concrete tray supported by columns or piers. The columns and trays can be preconfigured to allow for the design of new structures and uses below the new landscape. This concept has been used in many "air rights" projects where highways and railways are bridged over in such a way as to allow for the creation of a new cityscape, reconnecting the two previously disconnected sections of a city.

The "Breda Sands" proposal by Monolab, a satellite town outside Breda, the Netherlands, looks like a landscape from afar. Its gently rolling grasslands and dunes are in fact raised planes of concrete platforms covered with vegetation. This rolling landscape of concrete, grass, sand, and water is occasionally sliced with canyon-like chasms, which bring light deep into the interior of buildings below the concrete platform.

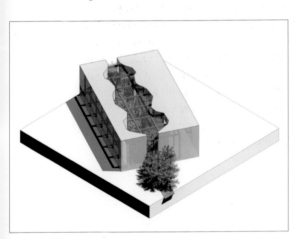

23

Green within Buildings

The natural and man-made environments coexist in new building configurations, where the distinction between green and occupied spaces are ambiguous and overlapping. A courtyard building for instance, is a classic example of this concept. The courtyard's more private spaces are organized around a green courtyard. More radical examples such as the Commerzbank in Frankfurt or the extraordinary towers by Yeang Architects, demonstrate how landscape can be interwoven with interior

and exterior public spaces in a skyscraper. Nature and technology merge and intertwine in complex spatial configurations.

24

Carving Volumes out of Green

Creating distinct separations between landscape and built spaces can help define the domains of each, while protecting nature from unwanted encroachments. The Indian settlement of Mesa Verde in southwestern United States is an example of a community that shaped its space and habitat out of the natural rock formations. The original settlers to the United States often carved out space for their communities from the wild forests.

25

Buildings as Green Berms and Land Forms

Buildings constructed of trays of landscape with inhabited uses below can be stacked and offset so as to create landscape-like forms of any kind. The simplest configuration would be building as berm, where one side of the building consists of offset trays of landscape with large expanses of glass overlooking terraced gardens. The other side of the building might be more conventionally configured, having typical wall systems defining its outer skin, looking much like any standard building. This building type is useful in shielding unattractive views of industrial uses or infrastructure, while allowing the building to tie into a variety of urban and natural contexts.

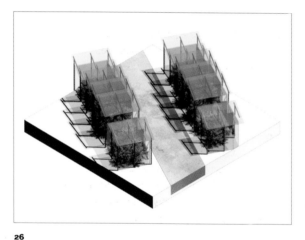

26

Encasing Nature

Where the climate is extreme, intensive zones of nature can be contained in large glass enclosed structures. These structures can also provide a welcome reprieve in more urban settings from pollution. These structures can be used to grow food, flowers, and even trees. These building types can also serve as a kind of infrastructure, serving as a shared public space for adjacent structures. A series of these structures, each linked by walkways, can be the genesis of a new suburban fabric.

Examples of such projects range from the practical to the utopian. Greenhouses, botanical gardens, office atriums, and "winter gardens" in dense urban centers provide a reprieve from our everyday environments. More exuberant architectural examples include Sir Nicholas Grimshaw's design of enormous bulbous greenhouse structures in England. John Todd's "arks" were self-sustaining dwellings that provided living space and produced their own energy and food, including fruits, vegetables, fungi, and fish.[6]

Taming Parking

The management of parking remains one of the most difficult problems facing the land-use patterns of suburbs and edge cities. Accepting that, the car as a concept representing personal mobility will be with us in some form or another, for some time. What options exist for mitigating the impact of the car, in particular parking, on the environment? The design of parking structures has advanced considerably as parking structures are combined with other uses and even landscape elements (natural paving, recycled materials, etc.). And then there are the numerous experiments into new kinds of mobility systems and their delivery mechanisms, where the very concept of "car" is challenged. These include the Segway, and the MIT Concept Car, which can be stacked when parked so as to limit its footprint.

27

Green Parking Fields

Developing "Green Parking Fields" is a strategy designed to mitigate the negative environmental consequences that large parking fields present, both to the health of the ecosystem and its aesthetic quality. By dividing the parking fields into 60-foot wide swaths, trees can be planted between rows of parking. Not only does this visually transform a gray parking field into something much greener and more pleasant to the eye, but it also helps absorb storm water runoff, provides shade, and reduces the heat island effect. In addition, perforated concrete pavers can be used to allow grass to grow on the parking surfaces. As the trees grow more majestic and grand in scale, "parking" will transform to "park."

29

28

Compressed Parking

Over one-third of the area required to support parking lots is designated for circulation. While gracious in dimension, the space designated for circulation is costly, especially as land becomes more valuable. In New York City and other dense metropolitan areas, parking lots squeezed between buildings maximize their revenues by double- and triple-parking their cars. Rows of cars, bumper to bumper, allow attendants to pack in cars efficiently. Similar systems are used by auto rental agencies at airports. Thus, through the improved space management and retrieval mechanisms of cars in lots (aided by digital tools), the size of parking lots could be dramatically reduced.

On-street parking is another form of compressed parking commonly used in the city—but not in the suburbs—as the road serves a dual function: street movement and access for parking. Consequently, lots of space can be saved, reducing the demand on conventional parking fields.

Vertical Parking

Vertical parking is another term for a parking garage, yet its design potential is only now being fully explored. While the scale and vastness of parking garages can be intimidating, narrower and more compact designs allow light to penetrate interior spaces and make these smaller structures feel safer. The facades of a structure can be integrated into surrounding contexts, challenging the traditional negative connotations of parking structures. Other uses such as ground floor retail and even museums can be combined with this building type. Also, where the terrain slopes, parking can be tucked beneath the sloping grade, shielding it from public view.

Robotic parking systems for instance, allow for even more densely compacted parking arrangements, as parking spaces are tightly stacked vertically and accessed through mechanical and digital means. While the equipment is costly, its expense can be offset in contexts where land costs are prohibitive.

Endnotes

1   Hans Ibelings, *The Artificial Landscape* (Rotterdam: NAI, 2000) 43.
2   See Andres Duany, Elizabeth Plater-Zyberk and Jeff Speck, *Suburban Nation: The Rise of Sprawl and the Decline of the American Dream* (New York: North Point Press, 2000) 24.
3   Rem Koolhaas, *Delirious New York: A Retroactive Manifesto for New York* (New York: Monacelli Press, 1995).
4   William Mitchell, *E-topia: Urban Life, Jim—But Not as We Know It* (Cambridge, Mass.: MIT Press, 1999) 13.
5   Mark Benedict and Ed McMahon, *Green Infrastructure: Linking Landscape and Communities* (Washington, D.C.: Island Press, 2006) 258.
6   Nancy Jack Todd, *A Safe and Sustainable World* (Washington, D.C.: Island Press, 2005).

Chapter 7

Spatial Models

Developing a strong spatial model, a system of complimentary building and landscape typologies that are organized around a larger set of principles about the distribution of public and private space and their distribution in a city's fabric, can contribute to creating a unique sense of place in suburban communities. This is evident in memorable cities and towns, whether it is found in the grid of Manhattan, Washington, D.C.'s long avenues, or the white clapboard public buildings and residences clustered around a New England common.

Suburbs on the other hand, lack strong spatial models and are organized around generic building types and spatial organizations that vary little in type regardless of region or locale. The same types of malls, office structures, and tract housing are tethered together by nondescript access roads, parking lots, and cul-de-sacs. It is rare that one can recreate from memory a cognitive map of an edge city or suburban community that is distinctive and compelling. Spatial models that reflect community visions are needed to transform edge cities and suburbs, and play a significant role in determining the overall order of a place and subsequent decisions about its evolution and transformation.

The following scenarios illustrate but a few of the infinite types of available spatial models. Developing a scenario is like doing a quick sketch of an idea but over a longer period of time. It provides a degree of freedom in testing the fit between a spatial model and its potential to match the needs of a community, given its existing conditions and parameters. Six spatial models were tested on the Burlington site: bridging infrastructure, creating a core, parallel streams, natural and built strips, anchoring objects, and stitching suburban fabric. Each scenario consists of a "filmstrip" comprised of multiple "frames" that are organized around five thematically defined vignettes.

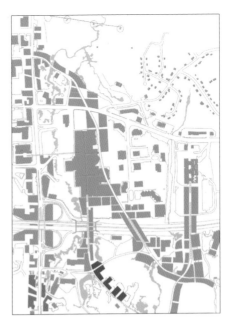

Scenario One: Bridging infrastructure

Scenario Two: Create a core

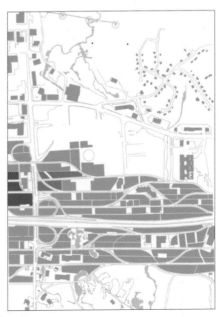

Scenario Three: Parallel streams

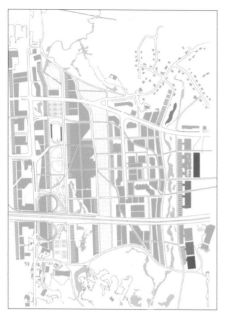

Scenario Four: Natural and built strips

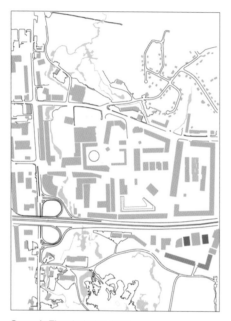

Scenario Five: Anchoring objects

Scenario Six: Stitching suburban fabric

Scenario One:
Bridging Infrastructure

Multilane feeder roads and other forms of infrastructure bisect suburbs physically, presenting barriers to pedestrians, bikers, and even cars and they divide communities socially. Bridging infrastructure can repair physical and social divides by connecting residents and workers to destinations within and beyond a community.

This scenario considers the potential of quite literally bridging the great divide created by Route 128, separating the southern and northern boundaries of Burlington. It builds on the strengths of existing pedestrian and traffic corridors and extends these routes to connect to the network of roads on the southern side of the highway. Bridging over the highway, and tunneling under it, strengthening connections. These connections serve as armatures for future development. Clusters of development crystallize at new intersections, shaped by new roads and their intersections with the existing network. Some of the new roadway configurations trace the geometry of past roadways. This occurs only where the trace of the road serves a "useful" contemporary purpose. Where it does not, the road deviates as needed to meet current programmatic needs. Those needs are imagined to be consistent with the types of uses that currently occupy the site, with the exception of adding higher concentrations of housing. Townhouses, lofts, and apartments mix with retail and corporate development. The presence of the natural landscape is reasserted through its reconstruction in locations corresponding to formerly paved-over aquifers and waterways.

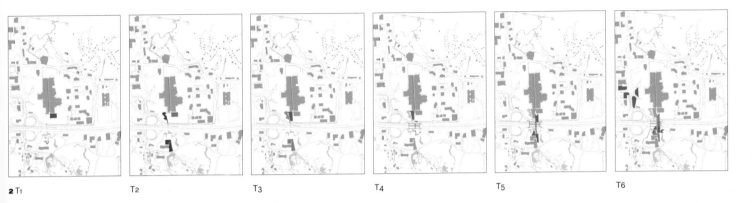

2 T₁   T₂   T₃   T₄   T₅   T₆

Vignette 1

The mall's central spine is extended, connecting it to
Wheeler Road to the south. A tunnel is excavated under
Route 128. Additional retail is built alongside the spine,
connecting to a hospitality and conference center on
Wheeler Road. Lost landscapes of wetlands and forests
are reestablished adjacent to this new spine.

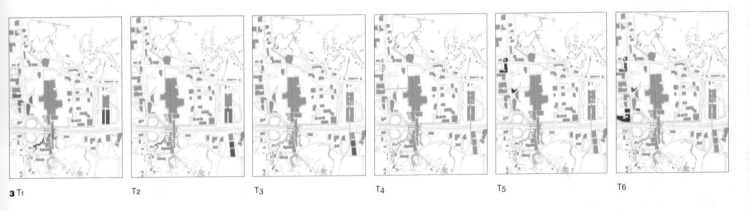

3 T₁   T₂   T₃   T₄   T₅   T₆

Vignette 2

A strong link between Lahey Clinic and the existing
cluster of corporate headquarters on the south
side of the highway improves vehicular and pedestrian
access. Extending a new addition along its current
circulation spine adds badly needed space to the clinic.
In subsequent frames this expansion anchors a new
pedestrian bridge.

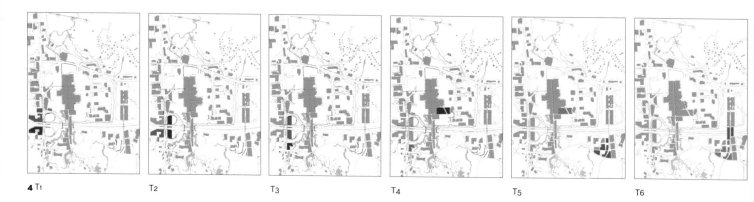

4 T1   T2   T3   T4   T5   T6

Vignette 3

Further concentrations of development are created
along Middlesex Turnpike including inside interchange
cloverleafs. Small-scale bridges and tunnels, which
minimize the presence of the highway as a divider,
bridge north and sound ends of the development.
Later frames witness additional development along the
Turnpike and recently constructed spines in Chapters
1 and 2.

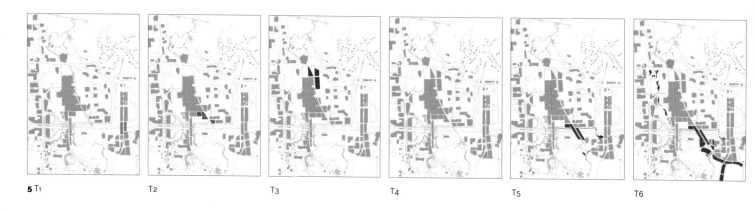

5 T1   T2   T3   T4   T5   T6

Vignette 4

The trace of an old road linking Woburn to Billerica
serves as the basis for a new link across the highway. It
connects the Burlington Mall Road to the north with
Wheeler Road to the south. In frame T5, a significant
bridge is constructed with buildings saddled alongside it.

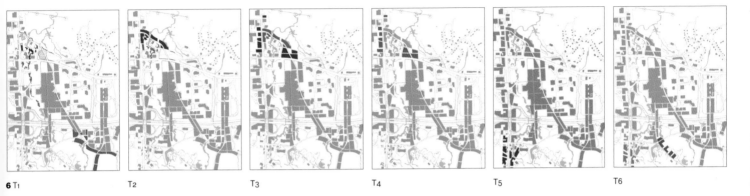

6 T1   T2   T3   T4   T5   T6

Vignette 5

The final vignette extends corridors of development along existing and new roads. The first frames concentrate development at the intersection of the Middlesex Turnpike, Burlington Mall Road, and parcels adjacent to the conservation lands. The lost landscape is reconstructed and bounded by new housing developments and live-work spaces. The middle frames further strengthen the definition of the street edge along the southern portion of Middlesex Turnpike. The last frames focus on extending the mall.

By the final frames of this scenario, Burlington's fabric of buildings and open spaces takes on a more organic feel, not dissimilar to a network of smaller villages. Large, medium, and small structures are clustered in consistent patterns of built and open spaces to create a richly varied texture. The highway, like a mighty river tamed by bridges spanning its girth, is intertwined with a new fabric of buildings and landscape.

7

Scenario Two:
Creating a Core

Many edge cities are widely dispersed and lack an identifiable center, that highly prized mix of businesses, residences, shops, restaurants, public spaces, and walkable streets that is so important economically and socially. Crossroads are treated merely as highway interchange and Main Street does not exist having been supplanted by the strip.

Without relying on traditional New Urbanist's idioms, this scenario speculates on the possibilities of creating a dense core development in and around the major highway cloverleaf intersection serving most of Burlington's edge city. Construction intensifies along two axes: the highway's edge and along Middlesex Turnpike. This infill strategy of building along existing roads establishes them as a downtown, or center, and protects outlying lands from further development. It also avoids the cost of laying down miles of new pipe and asphalt. Density is key to the economic success of public transportation. It is a central component of this scenario, and proposes the construction of a new transit spine—rail or bus—along Route 128, connecting Burlington with other suburban centers. This improved regional transportation system is complimented, as in many large airports, by a new network of pedestrian ways and moving sidewalks. A new kind of node is created, vibrant and connected.

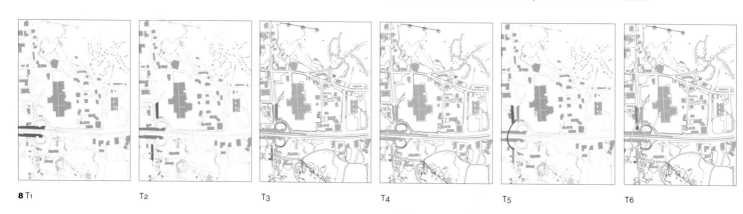

8 T1   T2   T3   T4   T5   T6

Vignette 1

The beginnings of a public transportation system (bus or rail) are established alongside the Route 128 overpass and its intersection with the Middlesex Turnpike. Two platforms are built with pedestrian access provided from below. This investment of public infrastructure spurs

further development along the Middlesex Turnpike.
Pedestrian networks (shown in yellow) are developed to
connect old and new developments.

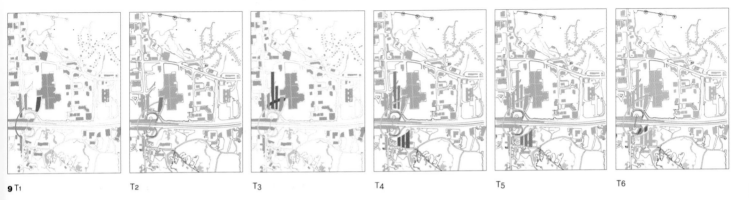

9 T₁   T₂   T₃   T₄   T₅   T₆

Vignette 2

The oval-shaped pedestrian network serves as the armature for new developments of office, retail, live-work, and
other uses concentrated in the vicinity of the cloverleaf
intersection. Linear building types, allowing for access
to natural light, are splayed between existing roads and
buildings to create the beginnings of a more continuous
and directional fabric.

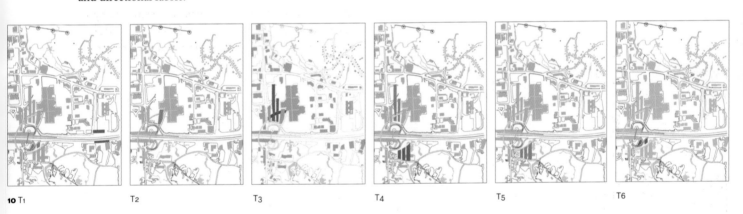

10 T₁   T₂   T₃   T₄   T₅   T₆

Vignette 3

Construction running parallel to the highway begin
to take shape in this vignette. They are organized along
two series of moving sidewalks. Long linear buildings
run along these systems and as the density of buildings
and people increases, additional stops and cross-
routes are added. Later, an additional oval circumscribes
the original.

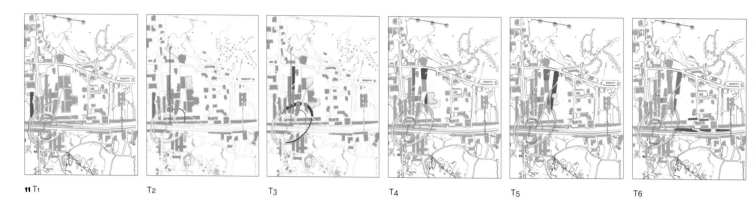

11 T1   T2   T3   T4   T5   T6

Vignette 4

Connections between the linear and oval systems strengthen as additional secondary systems are added. New structures grow along these new secondary networks. As the site density increases, several buildings are "erased" and their uses are relocated in configurations more in keeping with the site's evolving morphology.

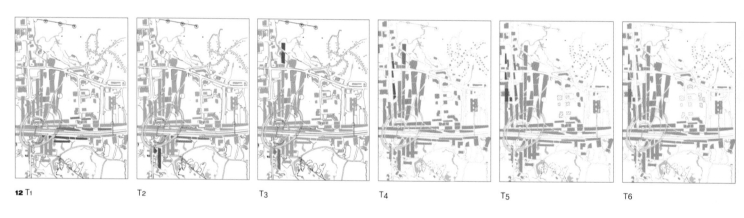

12 T1   T2   T3   T4   T5   T6

Vignette 5

As developments continue to intensify the "edges" alongside Middlesex Turnpike and the highway, the existing speculative offices at "New England Office Park" have been largely relocated. This allows for the erasure of most of the office park, and the creation of new or reclaimed landscape in their place. Buildings along the highway shield sound, making this office "park" a quiet and desirable destination for the emerging community.

A new and identifiable core develops around the newly constituted regional and local public transit systems. The redistribution of buildings allows for a less dissipated land-use configuration and creates concentrated edges of development along the two major existing arteries. This frees up more interior land, which can now be converted to parks and open space.

Scenario Three:
Parallel Streams

This spatial model involves a radical reconfiguration of the highway on- and off-ramp system. The pattern is based in part on the research into alleviating traffic congestion by traffic engineers MVRDV, a Dutch architectural firm. Traffic typically clogs at off-ramps due to abrupt shifts in velocity. A more effective option would be to have a series of parallel off-ramps, each one leading to a slightly slower off-ramp. This would help dampen abrupt velocity shifts, minimizing traffic jams by creating a smoother traffic flow. The highway takes on a new configuration, resulting in a series of parallel lanes, each with its own designated speed, and on- and off-ramps. This scenario tests this idea and explores its potential for creating a suburban fabric.

The new road pattern yields many narrow strips of land between lanes, which can be occupied by a variety of buildings and open spaces. The building typologies will be long and narrow, and require bridges to create a secondary network of lateral connections between parcels and buildings.

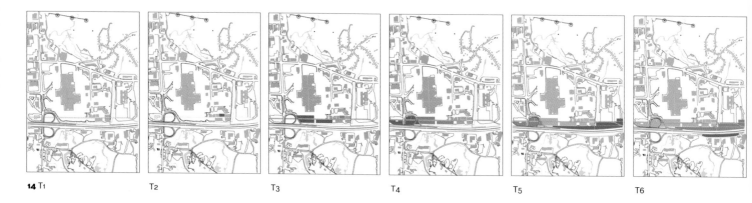

     T2   T3   T4   T5   T6

Vignette 1

The first frames show a new off-ramp on the north side of the highway. New parcels are created and infilled with smaller buildings. Eventually larger linear structures are pinched between the current highway and the feeder road. Buildings begin to fill in the voids of the cloverleaf. On the opposite side of the highway, minor alterations and demolition prepares for the construction of another new off-ramp.

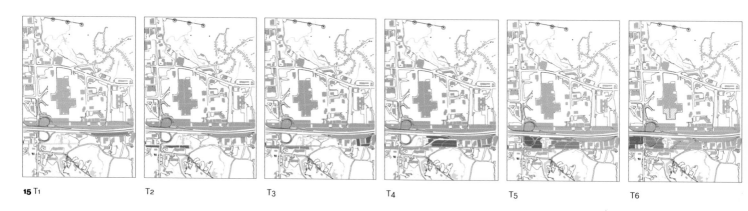

15 T1   T2   T3   T4   T5   T6

Vignette 2

The same patterns of feeder roads are extended on the south side of the highway. Incrementally, roads are positioned where they can squeeze between existing buildings, roads, and landscapes. Gradually, these parallel roads are connected with on- and off-ramps. Wherever possible, the landscape is preserved or enhanced through its reclamation.

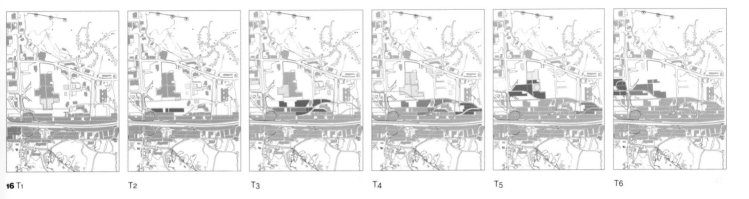

16 T1   T2   T3   T4   T5   T6

Vignette 3

A major new feeder road weaves through the Lahey
Clinic complex, office park, and the mall. Part
of the mall is "amputated" to accommodate the new
road. New buildings begin to inhabit these parcels,
complementing the geometry and shapes of the
remaining existing structures. Eventually the mall is
completely reconfigured and integrated as part of a
new road system.

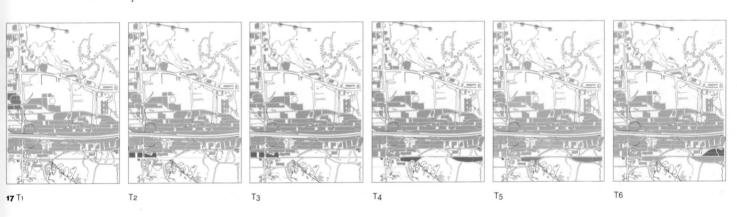

17 T1   T2   T3   T4   T5   T6

Vignette 4

The south side of the highway goes through a final iteration of road building as one more parallel feeder road is
built, slicing across some existing historic roads. These
curvilinear roads are largely integrated into the system of
on- and off-ramps. Once again, parcels are infilled with
new structures.

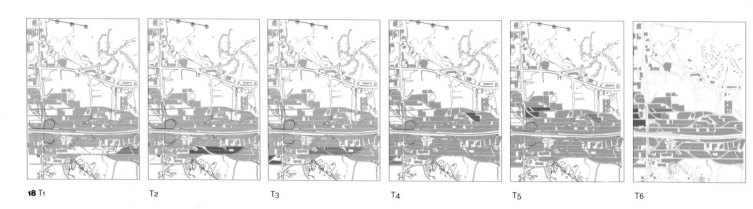

18 T1   T2   T3   T4   T5   T6

Vignette 5

Higher density is added to sites close to the highway, both to maximize the land use of the newly created parcels and to help shape a network of figural spaces. These areas are intended to create a variety of spaces, some containing landscape, others targeting more urban uses.

This is meant to be a radical proposal, but it must be understood in relationship to its regional implications. This typology ultimately yields a continuous linear city built along highways and roadways. While such a development pattern could result in carpeting a potentially homogenous linear metropolitan fabric, its benefit lies in concentrating development in a confined "highway swath" thereby protecting the landscape outside the swath.

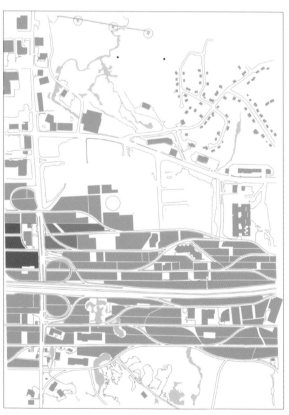

19

Scenario Four:
Natural and Built Strips

Clear zoning guidelines regulate and generate the distribution of buildings, and open spaces, and the way that they are used. Derived in part from the latent order of roads perpendicular to the highway and the buildings positioned in relationship to these roads, this scenario gives form to existing development patterns defining a new spatial pattern, organized along alternating strips of built to natural spaces. Within this alternating rhythm resonate more subtle ordering devices. Housing always contains the building zones, so that the housing always faces open space on one of its sides. Yet each built zone has a different concentration of uses: entertainment/cultural, retail, work, health, and so on. Similarly, the "green strips" change thematically from recreational playing fields, to farming/gardening, to conservation lands. The selection of each use is often based on the predominance of programs or clues already found within the boundaries of the strip. As automobiles speed along the highway, the rhythm of the built and natural strips will be legible, and will change along the length of the highway, both in content and measure, as site and circumstance dictates.

Concept

This proposal is based on zoning the existing site into alternating strips of built and natural environments. Each built strip is organized thematically around programs (entertainment, retail, office, and health); yet housing units always bound the "natural" strips.

20 T1   T2   T3   T4   T5   T6

New theaters, cafes, clubs, galleries, and related programs are added to the Middlesex Turnpike "Strip's" existing restaurants, bookstores, and movie theaters to create a new kind of linear entertainment/cultural zone.

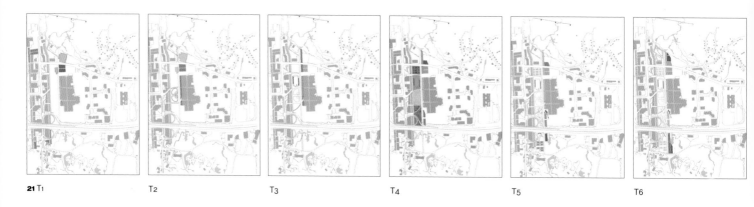

21 T₁   T₂   T₃   T₄   T₅   T₆

The former mall parking lots are converted to recreational playing fields (baseball, tennis, soccer, etc.), with structured parking below. Both sides of the fields are bounded by housing.

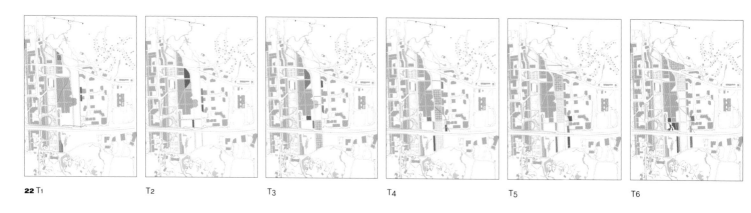

22 T₁   T₂   T₃   T₄   T₅   T₆

The mall's retail uses are expanded and reconfigured along the north-south axis. Paths and streets are cut laterally through the mall at strategic and/or historically significant locations.

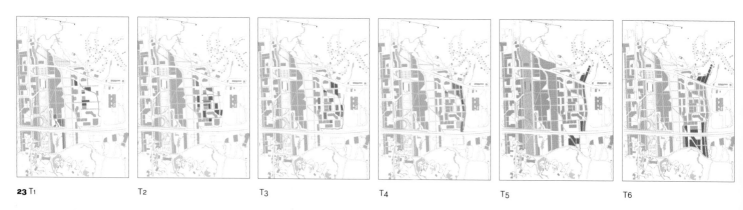

23 T₁   T₂   T₃   T₄   T₅   T₆

The parking lot to the east of the mall is converted into a "community farm" with housing on either side.

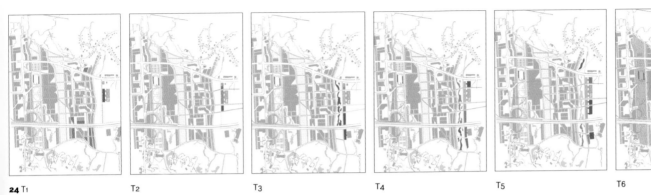

24 T1   T2   T3   T4   T5   T6

The office park is densified with additional office/parking structures. A network of ground level restaurants and shops are interwoven with a fabric of small plazas and parks.

The last natural "strip" is organized along the newly reconstituted streams and forests. This strip is bounded to east by the expanded Lahey Clinic facility.

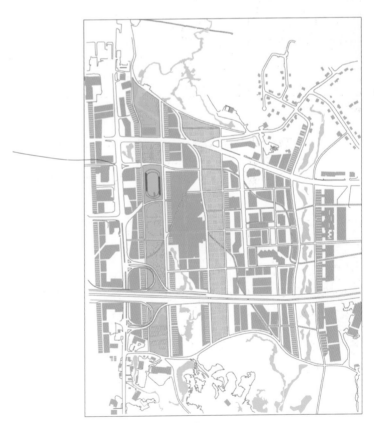

25

Scenario Five:
Anchoring Objects: The Greek Ideal

One of the masterpieces of Hellenistic urban design, Pergamon, located on a mountaintop in Asia Minor, is comprised of two building types. One is the bar building (the stoa), the other a box (the temple). Yet through the extraordinary and sensitive placement of these building types in relationship to one another and the landscape, their builders were able to create a rich and subtly modulated range of spaces.

The strip mall is a crude typological equivalent of a stoa, while the fast-food restaurant, the retail outlet, or office building ironically mimic the object-like quality of the temple. This scenario demonstrates how these two simple forms, the bar and the box, can create a tremendously rich array of spaces. By creating clearly defined—often courtyard-like—exterior space, bounded by stoa-like elements, object-like buildings can be strategically located within these spaces, so as to create spatially dynamic spaces, with strong visual relationships to adjacent sites and landscapes.

Concept

Finding inspiration in the designs of ancient Hellenistic cities such as Pergamon, this proposal utilizes two building types, the bar building (stoa) and the box (the temple). By bending and twisting the bar buildings (the strip mall typology), spaces can be bound and anchored to a site. The spatial configurations generated from the interplay of object and bar building are rich and unlimited.

26 T1   T2   T3   T4   T5   T6

The space around the mall's food court is excavated, so as to liberate the food court's circular shaped form. This process of erasure provides a clearer definition of the courtyard that bounds the food court.

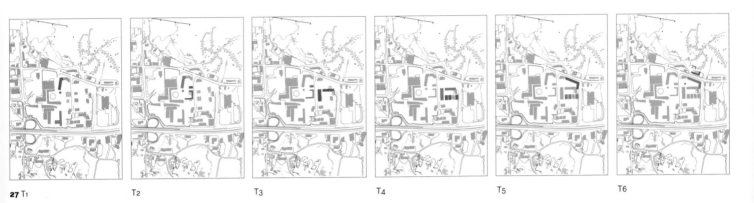

27 T₁   T₂   T₃   T₄   T₅   T₆

New (bent) bar buildings to the northeast of the food
court shape a series of courtyards that link the western
extents of the office park with the mall. The shapes of
the courtyard spaces are strategically positioned to create reciprocal relationships between adjacent courtyard
spaces. This same pattern of courtyards parasitically engages the office park.

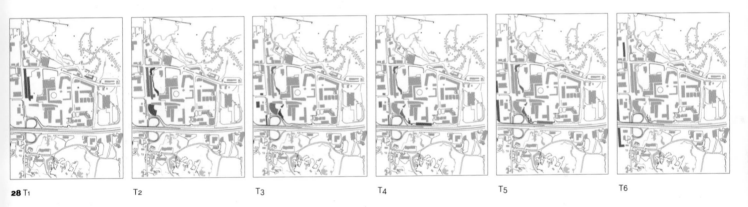

28 T₁   T₂   T₃   T₄   T₅   T₆

The edges of the Middlesex Turnpike are bounded by
a pair of bar buildings that help define the newly reclaimed streams and wetlands to the west of the mall. A
new theater is nestled alongside the inner bend of the
highway's off-ramp.

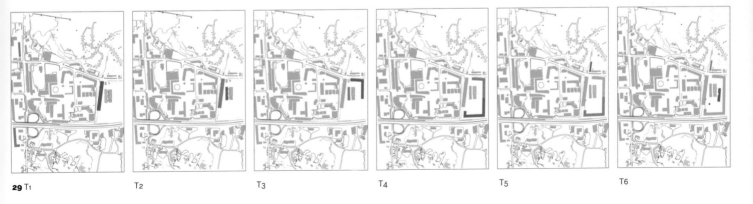

29 T₁   T₂   T₃   T₄   T₅   T₆

Lahey Clinic's object-like structure is bounded by a series of bar-like structures to help define its own precinct.

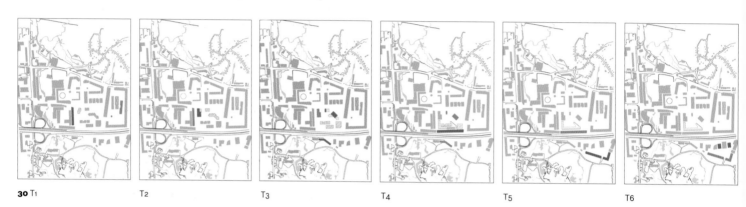

30 T₁   T₂   T₃   T₄   T₅   T₆

Further incremental small scale interventions help give clearer spatial definition to open spaces and courtyards in the office park.

The same building and spatial typologies are extended over the highway, adjusting their geometry and use based on local circumstance.

31

Scenario Six:
Stitching Suburban Fabric

This scenario illustrates a more conventional approach and relates strongly to New Urbanist dictums. It proposes a viable strategy for creating a fabric that is suburban in character. The sizes of the building units that comprise this fabric's texture are derived from the size, scale, and configuration of building types found in current suburban contexts. They include big boxes, speculative office buildings, as well as low-rise strip developments. What differs though is the location of these elements in relationship to one another. They are positioned so as to strengthen the edges along major roads. They bound newly created spaces and plazas, and they are strung together to generate a continuity of building mass along streets. Streets link spaces to other spaces and are conducive to wayfinding. This fabric is less about the parts (the individual buildings) than about the whole.

Concept

This scenario illustrates a more conventional and highly viable strategy for creating a fabric that is suburban in character. Buildings define spaces and streets, and spaces and streets are in turn linked to a legible neighborhood fabric. This fabric is less about the parts (i.e., the individual buildings) than about the whole that is created through the careful positioning of its constituent parts.

32 T1   T2   T3   T4   T5   T6

Smaller office buildings are infilled between existing offices at the office park. Residentially scaled commercial and housing structures bound Mall Road and extend northward towards the tract housing developments.

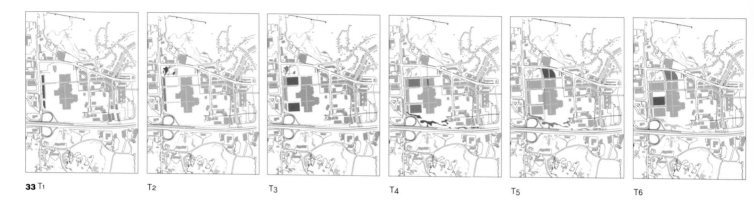

33 T1   T2   T3   T4   T5   T6

"Big box" retail structures are built adjacent to the existing mall, creating a series of new roads and open spaces.

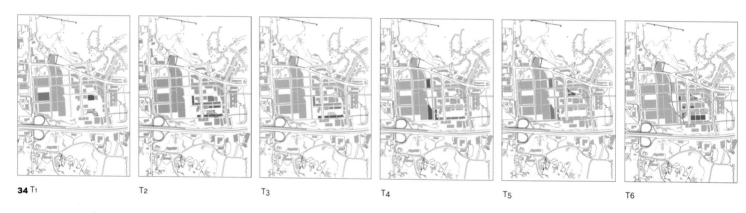

34 T1   T2   T3   T4   T5   T6

The parking spaces between the mall and the office park are overlaid with a new grid network of paths, streets, and new buildings.

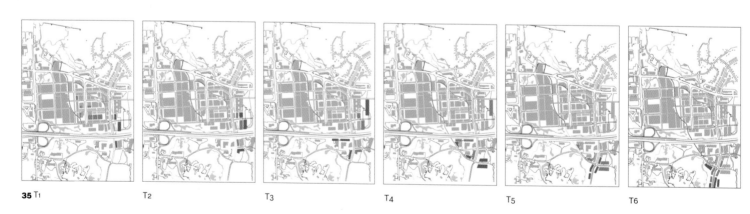

35 T1   T2   T3   T4   T5   T6

The office park's interior is inhabited with new multi-use structures, creating a dense fabric of spaces.

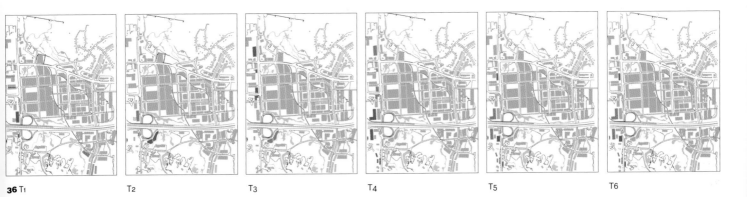

36 T1   T2   T3   T4   T5   T6

The fabric of streets, buildings, and spaces extend over the highway to envelope the fragmentary distribution of existing buildings.

The visual chaos of Middlesex Turnpike is converted into a more clearly defined streetscape with the addition of carefully positioned buildings.

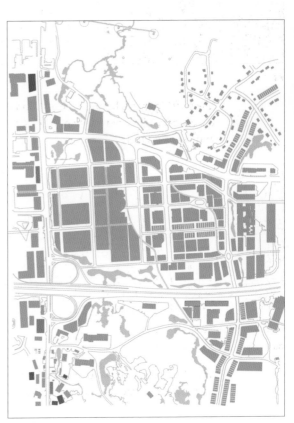

37

Burlington, Massachusetts

Projections

Every community arises out of different forces and circumstances and, as much as is possible, has the power to shape its future. Projections provide a means for generating different scenarios for a community's future and testing their viability in matching a vision with a community's goals, values, and resources. Scenarios can be based on clearly defined long-term strategic goals, supported by tactical plans, and strung together by a narrative. The narrative can be translated into images illustrating the physical transformation of a place. These images can be linked together, like a filmstrip, demonstrating how a community can change frame by frame. Each frame shows how the components of a community change, not only its built and natural elements, but potentially linking these transformations to economic, social, and policy-related criteria and data. Projections are a powerful tool in assisting communities in strengthening and transforming their identities.

2-4 Panoramas of Burlington

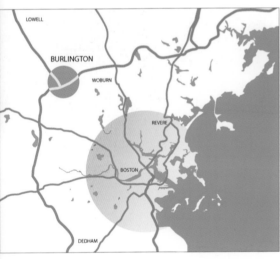

1 Locus map, greater Boston area

This chapter sets forth a hypothetical vision for Burlington that seeks to enhance its environmental quality, while remaining competitive as a marketplace, workplace, and residential community. A number of strategic guidelines are proposed, which take into consideration architectural, urbanist, ecological, and transportation issues:

→ Reestablish landscape presence and natural functions
→ Enhance recreational opportunities
→ Integrate uses with infrastructure where desirable
→ Provide strong pedestrian links
→ Mitigate the presence of the automobile
→ Support and nourish businesses and industries, the lifeblood of contemporary economies
→ Mix uses, including public and cultural uses, throughout the community to create vitality
→ Create landmarks and a system of orientation

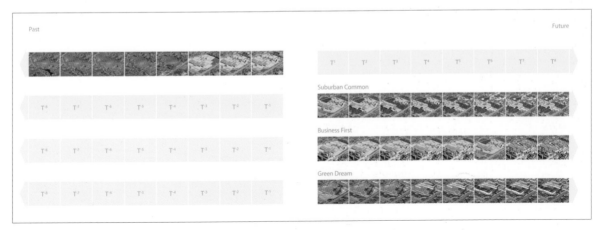

5 Analyzing Burlington's past [(T^{-8}) to (T^0)] and three potential scenarios for future transformation [(T^0) to (T^8)]

The desired result is a healthy community, where urbanity merges with arcadia, and the benefits of high technology support the complex interplay of natural, social, and economic systems. The car is accommodated, yet its negative effects are tamed. The continuous roar and hum of highway traffic is muffled by bermed buildings that run parallel to the banks of the highway. Parking fields are clustered, hidden, compressed, and always green and accessible to neighboring buildings and public spaces. Business thrives and has room to grow, burrowing into the earth and growing modestly skyward where necessary. Parcels for construction are not limited to the ground plane and its traditional two-dimensional definition; instead parcels are claimed on all surfaces elevated on rooftops or carved from the earth. Landscapes are constructed and altered through successive acts of addition and layering, like an ancient geological condition, where sedimentary layer upon layer is deposited. History is selectively revealed where a sectional profile is cut and sliced. With each new layer of transformation, the density of community experience is intensified, creating a labyrinthine construct, unique to site and the forces that generated its form.

The following eight frames represent chapters in the transformation of Burlington. In each frame, different tactical transformations are employed to achieve the community's strategic goals. The frames are based in part on an evaluation of the cross-maps, which highlight design opportunities and issues. Specific sets of design actions (each associated with a specific time frame) can be generated in response to each cross-map. The sequencing of tactical actions can be analyzed in terms of their effectiveness in achieving strategic goals. The sequences can be shuffled, edited, and modified dynamically over time to meet immediate as well as long-term objectives.

6 T₁

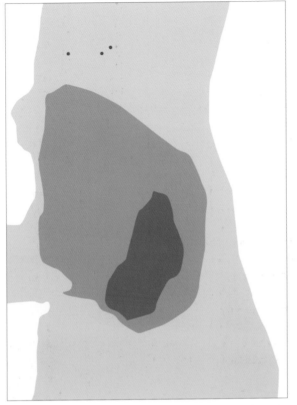

New "Green" parking
fields

Restored aquifer

7 Aquifer

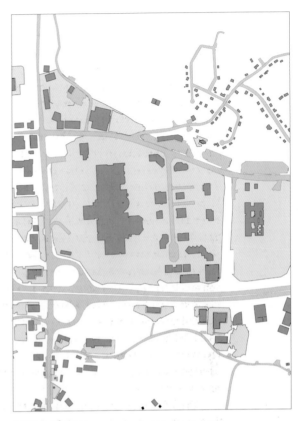

8 Asphalt surfaces

T1
Strategic Goal

Restore natural processes vital to protecting water
quality

Tactical Actions

Recreate the lost wetland over the high-yield aquifer
Tame existing parking fields with trees and porous
surface treatments

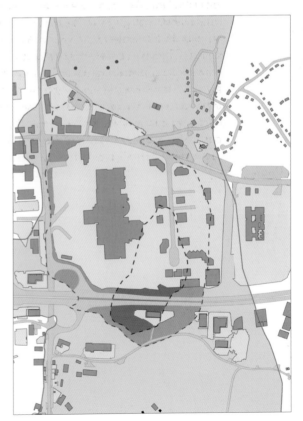

9 Cross-map = Aquifer + Asphalt

A cross-map overlaying underground water supplies with asphalt surfaces shows the extent to which recharge areas are blocked by parking lots. This is especially true in the parking areas located between the mall and the office park, where the largest capacity aquifer is located. Only a small portion of the southern boundary was left natural. The aquifer is unable to recharge; consequently its volume is diminishing, creating occasional sinkhole-like conditions in the parking lot. In addition, pollutants from the cars and salts from snow removal are seeping into the ground, presenting a danger to water quality. To protect underground water quality and quantity, the logical first step is to do something about the expansive parking lots.

Since it sits directly above the highest capacity aquifer, the lot between the mall and the office complex represents the best opportunity for enhancing ground-water recharge. Recreating a wetland in this area could restore natural processes that sustain aquifers including: storm water retention, purification, and percolation. A recreated wetland would consist of forested buffer strips, riparian vegetation, and surface water. Vegetation would need to be carefully selected and planted to ensure the desired natural services. Wildlife benefits should be considered and target species identified, since an opportunity may exist to connect populations that have been divided by human development. Ecologists play a key role in this transformation.

Since the new wetland envelops some of the office buildings, parking strategies must be rethought. Adjacent parking lots in the mall and office complex could be converted into compact parking parks. Besides moderating the extremes of climate, parking parks visually soften the stark environment created by the unmitigated presence of asphalt. Porous pavers and other surface webbing systems that incorporate grass and vegetation could improve infiltration to the aquifer, but would have to be used carefully to mitigate contamination from petroleum products.

10 T2

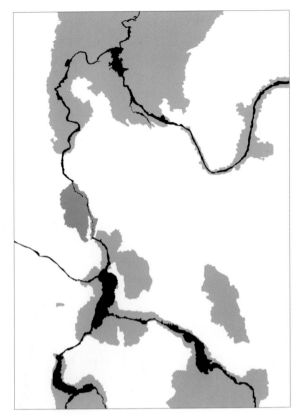

11 Historic wetlands and streams

12 Current wetlands and streams

-------- New artificial landscape

-------- Restoring stream corridor

T2
Strategic Goals
Reestablish landscape presence and natural functions
Enhance recreational opportunities

Tactical Actions
Recreate a stream corridor along Middlesex Turnpike
Build a new partial "artificial landscape" providing parks
    and parking

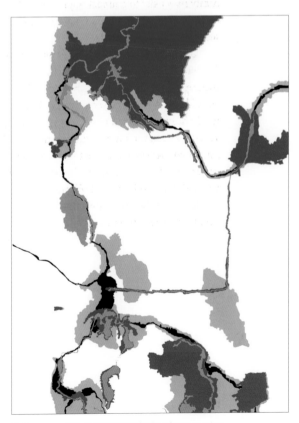

13 Cross-map = Historic + Current wetlands and stream system

An overlay of maps depicting the current and historic stream system reveals a significant disruption of the flow of natural ground water systems and supporting wetlands. The northern and southern portions of the site have been largely severed and a winding stream replaced by a drainage swale that follows a rigid geometry. The swale is comprised of two straight segments; a right angle turn keeps it within the easements and property lines. This most unnatural path serves to maximize the amount of surface parking and the build-out of the site, but diminishes recreational and ecological values.

This frame focuses on reconnecting the larger wetlands regions north and south of the mall. A stream corridor that runs parallel to the Middlesex Turnpike is created. Part of this new landscape is elevated and constructed as a new form of infrastructure that economically mediates the change in elevation between the higher levels of the Middlesex Turnpike and the currently depressed parking fields. Since it is elevated in places, it can extend the width of the corridor beyond the ground space available. The space created between the elevated artificial landscape and the current parking field can support structured parking.

The new stream cuts through the new infrastructure and forms a new kind of landscape, one related to, but not identical to, the historic landscape. Its banks consist of forested buffer strips and provide recreational amenities such as parks, fields, skating ramps, and playing fields. People congregate here during the lunch hour and weekends, and its mere existence will act as a welcome visual reprieve to current asphalt landscape.

14 T3

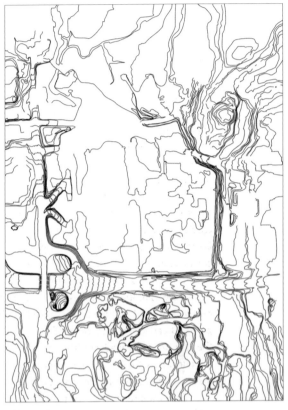

New bermed
landscape

Terraced
buildings

15 Noise levels

16 Topography

T3
Strategic Goals
Mitigate the automobile's presence
Support and nourish businesses and industries

Tactical Actions
Build bermed office and industrial structures to shield
    unwanted sound from the highway
Plant the terraces of the bermed structures with trees
    and vegetation

17 Cross-map = Noise level + Topography

The overlay of sound and topography highlights what appear to be obvious yet startling relationships between sound levels—measured in decibels—generated by the highway and the site's topography and buildings. Measurements taken more or less on a grid confirm that the highest noise levels are recorded close to the source of the sound, the highway.

These spaces are not desirable for most uses, and little public activity occurs in these areas. The open spaces are transitional only, supporting movement from car to mall or office.

Large tracts of underutilized land can be re-claimed for higher uses by mitigating noise. Large two- and three-story earth embankments could be built to contain highway noise and harbor office and industrial spaces within their volumes. Part landscape, part infra-structure, they would appear as landscape from the mall, but as conventional office buildings with three stories of glass from the highway. These structures line both sides of 128, and follow the eastern side of the Middlesex Turnpike. They embrace the current parking fields and convert the acoustical wasteland into a well-tempered environment suitable for public and recreational uses.

18 T4

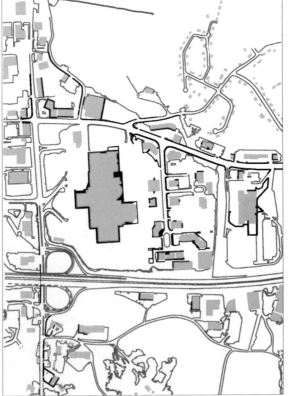

Improved pedestrian link

New hybrid structure

New bridge building
spans highway

19 Sidewalks

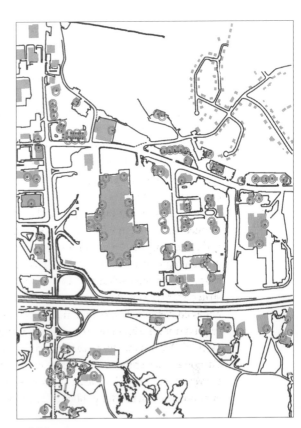

20 Building entrances

T4
Strategic Goals
Integrate uses with infrastructure
Provide pedestrian links

Tactical Actions
Augment and improve the existing pedestrian system
throughout the site
Build new hybrid structures that fill in and span voids
between existing office buildings
Span the highway with a new bridge-like building providing additional pedestrian access and connections

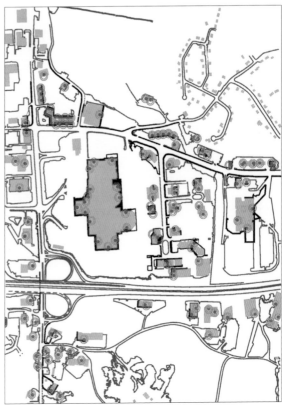

21 Cross-map = Sidewalks + Building entrances

Suburban communities are notoriously unwalkable and Burlington is no exception. While sidewalks do exist in many locations, their occurrence is haphazardly distributed along some roads, but not others. The Middlesex Turnpike and Mall Road both have sidewalks, but in many places sidewalks do not extend to buildings; pedestrians must cross large parking lots at their own risk. Not a single sidewalk links the major roads to the mall. Thousands of people traverse this landscape everyday, but the paths they take are determined by chance and are often treacherous.

A lack of relation between Burlington's building entrances and pedestrian walkways characterizes Burlington's existing weak fabric. A traditional, densely populated city has legible patterns of entrances, buildings, and streets. The buildings, their typologies, orientation, and entrances all contribute an urban fabric of unique character. Evident only occasionally in Burlington are consistent sets of relationships between buildings, their typologies, orientation, and entrances. The result is an urbanized landscape with none of the benefits of urban life (an active street life or cultural amenities), but all of its problems (traffic, increasing pollution, and rising property taxes).

While the beginnings of exterior figural spaces are created by some of the buildings in the office complex, they are the exception rather than the rule. A new building type overlaid onto the existing building fabric can create stronger spatial connections, while fostering a sense of community. This new typology has two basic configurations, one rooted to the ground and sandwiched between existing buildings, and the other parasitically anchored to the existing buildings' roofscapes while bridging buildings and voids. These buildings are strung together to link existing objects as part of a larger network of structures. This serves to create more direct connections between buildings, and also creates newly defined exterior spaces. Because some of the buildings are 40 to 50 feet above grade, they allow for important ground conditions, such as parks, roads, and "tamed" parking to remain in place.

In addition, a new bridge-like building over the highway connects the northern and southern segments of the community, allowing for improved pedestrian access. This new building rests on the bermed buildings on either side of the highway and connects to existing structures on either side of that great divide created by the highway.

22 T5

New housing for Lahey
-------- Clinic
-------- Interwoven landscape

-------- New housing

-------- New housing and offices

23 Property lines

24 Zoning

T5
Strategic Goal
Mix uses, including cultural uses, throughout the
   community to create a vibrant urbanity

Tactical Actions
Redistribute uses throughout the site
Add housing in proximity to the workplaces
Optimize the use of parking throughout the cycle
   of the day
Interject and weave landscape throughout the site

25 Cross-map = Property lines + Zoning

A by-product of segregating zoning districts into discrete areas is that each zone tends to be used intensively at one time of the day and then abandoned. For instance, the office park is fully occupied during normal working hours; however, after 6 p.m. the parking lot is empty, as all the employees depart en masse. This pattern creates an inefficient use of land because each person and his vehicle occupy a specific amount of space for a specific but limited time during the day. A designated parking space cannot serve multiple parties. In addition, traffic is aggravated, time lost, energy wasted, as people travel at the same time to similar destinations.

By redistributing the location of housing, from discretely defined zones to locations interspersed in the commercial districts, fewer car trips will be required to transport residents and employees between home and work locales. People may walk to work, stores, and parks, using their cars only when necessary. Traffic congestion can be greatly reduced. New housing around the Lahey Clinic would offer living quarters to busy interns and employees within walking distance of the hospital.

Distributing the office and retail uses around the entire site could also ease the need for parking. For instance, if some of the mall's smaller shops and office spaces were swapped, a parking space originally slated for one office worker between 9 a.m. and 5 p.m. could now serve a shopper in the after-work hours.

Finally, the landscape, now an area largely confined to conservation areas north and south of the mall complex, will be interwoven into the fabric of this community. Landscape, trees, and vegetation will find their way into every available piece of land, even on the tops of buildings and underneath new hybrid structures.

Work, shopping, living, and nature coalesce into a new urban order.

26 T6

-------- New multi-use parking
structure

-------- New green roof e-mall
-------- New parking fields

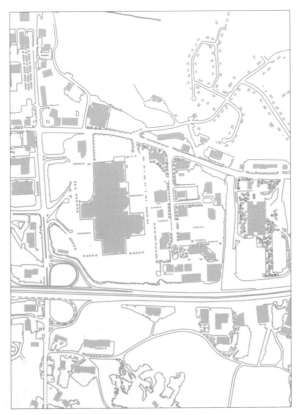

27 Planted trees

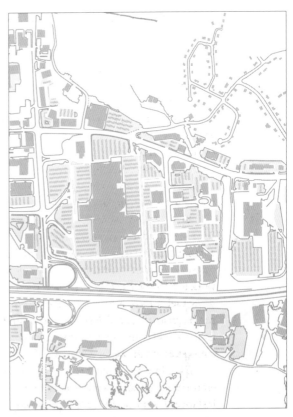

28 Parking fields

T6
Strategic Goal
Integrate uses with infrastructure

Tactical Actions
Consolidate parking in new structure, enveloped in
 public uses
Create a new roof landscape to cover both parking structures
 and the existing mall
Introduce new bermed parking structures where the
 topography allows for it
Create more clearly defined and bounded "rooms" containing
 parking fields
Connect these rooms to one another

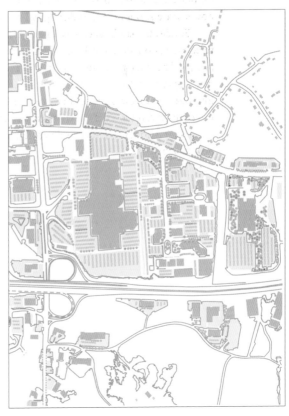

29 Cross-map = Planted trees + Parking

For the most part, a strong relationship between the shape of the parking and trees and the spaces they create does not exist. The exception to this observation is the central street in the office complex. In this boulevard-like setting, trees are arrayed on either side of the four-lane road. This boulevard, worthy of Paris, is visually anchored by an office tower directly on axis to the road. The road terminates in a vehicular turnaround with a water feature in its center.

As this site grows, the demands for parking can be addressed through the creation of a new hybrid building type, which will be comprised of parking, retail, and landscape. Located directly to the north of the existing mall, this structure will be wrapped on the east, west, and north elevations in retail uses, restaurants, and other amenities. The interior of this structure will contain multiple stories of parking, enough to accommodate the increased demand generated by the addition of program as well as make up for the parking lost to the reconstruction and creation of parks and woodlands. This new structure's roofscape could feature an energy farm integrated with photovoltaic cells and vegetation. This roofscape could extend over the existing mall as well.

Other, smaller "hybrid" interventions are provided throughout the site. These include the introduction of parking structures bermed into the earth (where the change in topography allows for it). Covering parking structures in landscape helps reduce their visual impact.

In addition, by strategically planting trees it is possible to create more clearly defined spaces. Bounding parking lots by trees can create more strongly defined room-like spaces, which in turn can be linked to other "rooms" of parking, creating a network of outdoor space.

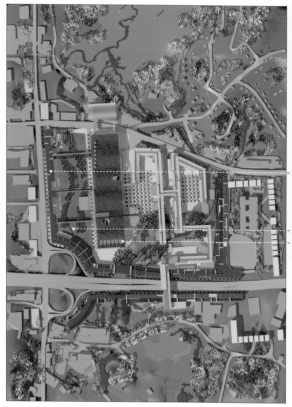

30 T7

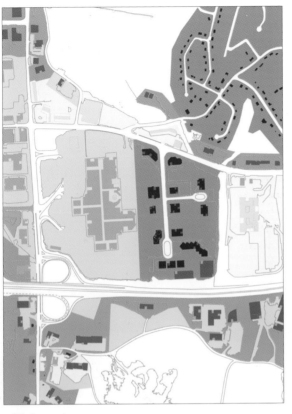

.... New multi-use buildings
        and cultural amenities

.... Recreational uses
.... New public amenities
        and uses

31 Private property

32 Public property

T7
Strategic Goals

Mix uses, including public and cultural uses, throughout
    the community to create a vibrant urbanity
Enhance recreational opportunities

Tactical Actions

Generate new multi-family housing units bordering
    existing conservation lands
Convert narrow parts of the conservation land into
    public accessible spaces
Reconfigure and enhance the shape and use of "left-
    over" public spaces along highways
Encourage and create incentives for private land-
    holders to engage in public activities

33 Cross-map = Private + Public property

Accessibility varies on both publicly and privately held lands. In the maps, the mall, a highly accessible area, is a lighter earth tone, while the office buildings, each with its own security guards standing in the lobby, are a darker tone. They are privately held spaces with limited access. Shades of blue mark public land that is highly accessible (light), and places where access is limited (dark). Remarkably little public land is truly public. Conservation lands, for example, are fenced off, and visible only from afar, their connection to the everyday lives of residents, workers, and visitors is limited. The only truly public space is a park located between the office complex and the Lahey Clinic.

The mall is a privately owned, quasi-public space. Despite its public image, the activities that take place within its boundaries are not truly public. Restrictions on activities and freedom of expression are determined by the management company's policies and enforced by its security staff. Any public acts of free speech or expression, supported by the constitution, are forbidden in this highly privatized environment raising important questions about the status of our public spaces in contemporary suburban environments.

Where can people congregate and express their ideas freely? Are public spaces just commercially oriented? The physical boundaries defining the conservation lands to the north and south of the mall could serve a valuable public role. Multi-family housing built adjacent to the conservation lands, but never violating their borders, could afford views of the conservation lands and its waterways. Low-impact uses could be programmed for the periphery of the conservation lands. These newly accessible spaces can be connected to other parks, creating a new network of park space.

Proposals should be entertained for reprogramming lost fragments of leftover land (often found next to highways, off-ramps, and easements). Land swaps with adjacent landowners can often yield newly configured property shapes that are mutually advantageous. Once these spaces are redefined, their accessibility and connections to existing pedestrian systems can be improved, turning a leftover space into an amenity. Negotiations with mall operators and private property owners can explore the possibility of programming a wider array of public uses and activities within privately controlled spaces.

34 T8

-------- Improved entrance to
the mall

-------- New Lahey clinic campus

35 Interior public spaces

36 Exterior figural spaces

T8
Strategic Goals
Create landmarks and a system of orientation
Provide pedestrian links

Tactical Actions
Create a campus around the Lahey Clinic
Construct a new tower on campus to serve as a land-
mark and means of orienting people
Reconfigure new entrances throughout the site to
correspond more directly with open public spaces
Strengthen the definition of existing public spaces
Create stronger visual relationships between spaces

37 Cross-map = Interior + Exterior spaces and entrances

Burlington, in its current condition, is comprised of many figural spaces where the intent behind the design of a space was driven by a variety of forces other than making them legible. The mall's parking lot is a good example of this phenomenon; where the mall is rectilinear, so are the adjoining parking lots. Trees planted between rows of parking create a series of spaces within the larger lot, analogous in some ways to the creation of rooms within a house. The relationships between these rooms can be deliberately determined or the result of happenstance. In Burlington, only the primary spaces created in the speculative office complex are anything other than random. Here, the intersection of the main two vehicular spines creates a strong spatial organization.

Activity zones during the span of the day give clues about the life of this place; in particular, the location of hot spots. Ideally, the figural spaces, their relative size and location, should correspond in patterns that reflect the ideal life of a community. Such patterns are in fact evident in the office complex, where the major entrances to the office buildings are aligned along the two primary axes. In fact, there are a cluster of entrances around the main square in front of the office tower, creating a hub of activity. This condition, though, is the exception to the rule. The mall's entrances, their location and size, have little do with the layout of the parking lot and its spatial configuration. They spill out into the lot, as the geometry of the mall's interior plan dictates. All the entrances are singular events, isolated from one another, lacking any kind of repetition or collective intent. This lack of definition creates a disorienting environment, requiring visitors to recalibrate their bearings by relying solely on signage, not all of which is readily visible, instead of developing a consistent system of landmarks and spaces.

Where possible throughout the site, major and minor entrances to buildings will be reconfigured so that there is a stronger relationship between the location of an entrance and an abutting public space. The location of entrances relative to one another will be taken into account to encourage the creation of a larger pedestrian-oriented network of entrances and spaces. This network will allow workers, residents, and shoppers to traverse the site more conveniently by foot, thereby reducing reliance on the car and activating public spaces.

The strategic planting of trees and vegetation can help create strongly defined spaces. Not only will these new room-like spaces be more enjoyable, but the carefully considered relationships between spaces will encourage the creation of a larger pedestrian network. The result is a town which is a garden, and a garden which is a town. A new symbiosis is generated where the structure and identity of both are inextricably intertwined.

Another opportunity on the site for creating figural spaces exists at the Lahey Clinic. The institution has landmark status, because of its scale and location, however the spaces around it do not match its grandeur. To meet its expansion needs, the clinic could become a campus with large public lawns, surrounded by new labs and housing. The complex could bridge over the highway to include some of the underutilized land to the south. The new public lawn, much like the lawn designed by Thomas Jefferson for the University of Virginia, is slightly raised above the existing grade level. Here it creates a more prominent landscape and conceals parking spaces beneath. In addition, a tower-like structure will be built on the south campus, and positioned in the middle of the lawn. This new tower provides a prominent landmark visible from the highway and around campus, helping people to orient themselves and adding a sense of scale and visual interest. The tower's significance is enhanced by its program, a research or administrative center.

Of special note is the relationship of the labs and residences to the lawn. The frequency of entrances will be increased as much as possible, and will be distributed along the perimeter of the lawn. This will help to enliven the public space with more pedestrian activity. The availability of housing on campus will help alleviate the demands on the traffic and parking, thereby reducing the cost of living for residents.

Recalibration

The transformation of Burlington will need to be recalibrated as construction and unforeseen events alter the community's landscape, financial needs, and overall goals. If the Lahey Clinic were to relocate outside Burlington, for example, the transformation of the city would require major modifications. A stagnant housing market, the introduction of mass transit, the decline of the mall, or increasing traffic on 128 might all call for recalibration. The dynamic recalibration of scenarios is important in allowing communities to change and adapt to changing circumstances.

38 Integrating infrastructure, landscape and development

39 Hybrid typologies engage the highway

Amsterdam, The Netherlands

Design concept by David Foxe

History

Nieuwe Meer, or "New Lake," is a place between places. The community gets its name from the lake it borders. Caught between Amsterdam's growing metropolitan area (whose center is six miles away) and Schiphol Airport (three miles away), which is fast becoming an urban nexus in its own right, Nieuwe Meer has entered into a period of intense suburban development.

Nieuwe Meer sits on the edge of the Haarlemmermeer, one of Holland's most historically significant polders, an area drained and reclaimed from the sea in the 1800s. The polder is six meters below sea level, while Nieuwe Meer is approximately one to two meters below sea level. A large elevated canal separates the topographic shift between these two terrains. The road leading to the historic village of Sloten, situated on the canal, provides a linear armature for the farmhouses strung along its length. Typical of the artificial Dutch landscape, water and roads are raised above the polders creating interesting cross-sections.

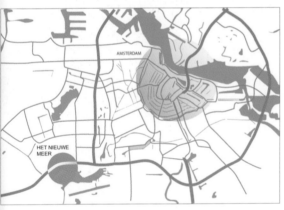

1 Locus map: Nieuwe Meer, Amsterdam

As Amsterdam's girth has expanded, especially over the last century, development pressures have manifested themselves on this delicate landscape. An Olympic stadium, completed for the games in 1928, occupies Nieuwe Meer's northeast flank. Adjacent housing communities designed by the Dutch architect Hendrik Petrus Berlage followed, as well as beautifully designed parks for rowing and sailing events. In the 1950s and 1960s a wave of Corbusian housing developments encroached on the larger district, taking advantage of easy vehicular access to Amsterdam, The Hague, and Rotterdam.

At the same time, Schiphol Airport, to the southwest, became a major international node for air travel. Continuous improvements to infrastructure networks (runways, railways, subways, and highways) and their integration with hotels, office buildings, corporate and retail centers, and cultural amenities, have generated a new kind of urban nexus around the airport. Its expansion directly impacts the Nieuwe Meer district in the form of increased noise, traffic, and development.

This patchwork quilt of reclaimed farmland, historic villages, corporate centers, intertwining infrastructure systems, and bucolic parkland is quickly becoming another generic suburb bisected by infrastructure and caught between two growing metropolises. What transformation patterns can be developed for this place between places to create a strong sense of identity that is uniquely tied to site and circumstance?

Analysis: Mapping

The survival of Holland has historically and even today been entirely dependant on water management. A country whose current profile is largely below sea level, Holland has developed a complex system of canals, dikes, and pumps (originally powered by windmills) to redirect water to higher elevations, leaving tillable soil for crops and suitable land for inhabitation. Water projects have been built at all scales, undertaken as national, regional, or local initiatives.

2 The Nieuwe Meer, a Dutch suburban landscape

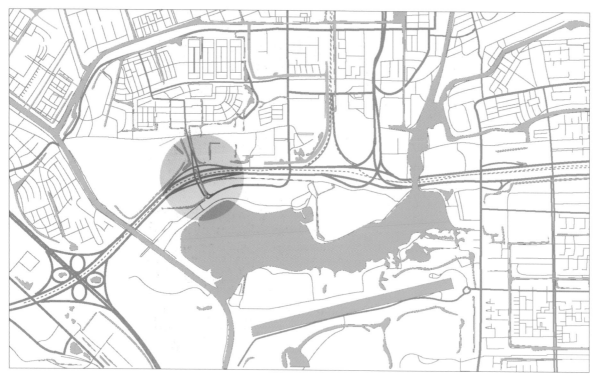

3 Canals and water systems

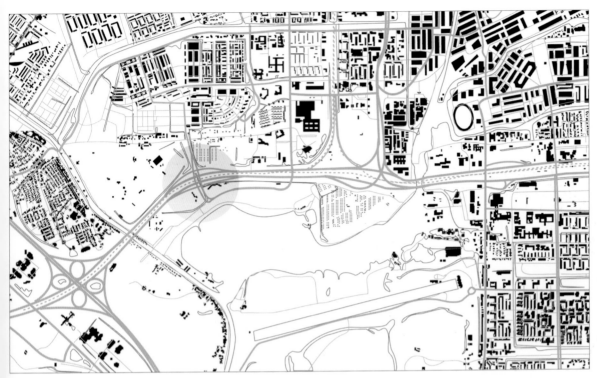

4 Building fabric

Traditionally, narrow strips of land bounded by canals improved the land's capacity to absorb water. The width and frequency of these parcels was a function of the land's capacity to absorb water, well understood by the farmers who tilled the soil. Small canals lead to large canals that in turn feed rivers and lakes, before ultimately heading seaward. The rich pattern of waterways and resulting landforms reveals the evolution of this landscape, and the sometimes opposing forces of hydrology and human settlement. Today, this pattern of waterways is disappearing as parcels are reconfigured to accommodate coarser-grained development patterns.

Buildings of all sizes can be found on Nieuwe Meer's figure ground plan in patterns that are equally as varied. The figure ground reveals their typology and placement within the context of larger historic patterns of development. For instance the clusters of small buildings strung along roadways are farm buildings, including the farmer's house, a barn, and ancillary structures which work within the limits of wooden spans and available plots of land. These have, over time, generated a densely woven fabric of buildings and courtyards.

5 Infrastructure

A larger parcel of plots on the north shore of the lake illustrates the Dutch penchant for creating "volkstuintjes," (or gardens for the people) where weekend gardeners can escape the city and cultivate lovely gardens in the midst of park-like settings. Small huts, deceptive in size, contain all the detail of larger villas, but at a fraction of the scale. This Arcadian utopia, finds itself in close proximity to a much coarser fabric of corporate complexes across the highway, whose size is determined by the optimized calculus of floor plate ratios, elevator capacities, building codes, and real estate market forces.

The search for new and modern forms has a rich tradition in modern Dutch architectural and planning history. Limited land dictates the need for higher density development patterns. A wide array of geometric patterns, reflecting the latest trends and tendencies amongst designers, generates efficient and habitable landscapes; some more successfully than others. Towers, slabs, townhouses come in all shapes and combinations. Some housing blocks are placed as free-standing objects in the landscape, others are linked by a well-defined system of streets and open spaces.

The idiosyncrasies of the site's history are also revealed by the aberrant military complex located next to the A4 highway, a leftover reminder of Schiphol's origin and military significance. Just east of this complex, a cluster of fast-food restaurants and motels typical of the nondescript architecture and inert typologies of strip development clutter the roadside.

The Oude Haagseweg, was the original primary road linking Amsterdam to The Hague. Its path, size, and direction varied as it negotiated the obstacles created by patterns of waterways. It runs parallel to the A4, which eclipsed it in the 1950s. Elevated on a berm as it passes through the Haarlemmermeer polder, the A4 has become a dike of sorts, but one that divides neighborhoods rather than tying them together, and demolishes anything it its path. It is a barrier built on a berm and crossed only by the occasional tunnel or bridge.

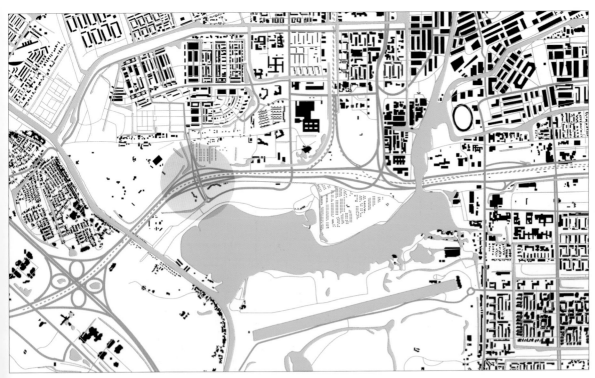

6 Waterways + Buildings

Cross-Maps

Historically, buildings followed the pattern of water-ways. They often ran alongside elevated canals, like the Haarlemmermeer, or perpendicular to them. All the rules change around the large corporate office and housing complexes, where the pattern of waterways is illegible and, in some places, has even been paved over.

7 Waterways + Infrastructure

Today recent modes of travel challenge the primacy of the canal system. Highways cut across the grain of the waterways, sometimes obliterating traces of connections between systems. However, as it crosses the canal near the Olympic stadium, the highway is integrated with canal, bike, and pedestrian paths. Each system serves its function in a balanced harmony with the others. This suggests a strategy for taming large-scale infrastructure.

Design

Nieuwe Meer is a site full of potential. Summer cottages, park spaces, sports fields, suburban housing, and the lakeshore could all be linked if harsh edge conditions were softened and the infrastructure tamed. Intensifying building patterns around infrastructure systems could ease development pressures in fragile landscapes. New typologies could draw on the traditional Dutch penchant for creating artificial landscapes and hybrid typologies where building, infrastructure, and landscape are integral to one another.

8 T1

9 T2

T1

Dividing and conquering the highway and rail lines makes the highway and rail lines more inhabitable and permeable to pedestrian and bicycle traffic.

T2

An elevated wedge-shaped canal extends the reach of the lake, bringing water into the zone where highway, sports fields, cottages, and suburban development come together. In an interesting twist on Dutch hydrological practice, land is erased to create a landmark that provides orientation for future development, defines public spaces, and links to the lake again areas previously cut off by the highway.

10 T3

11 T4

T3

Two new housing towers on either side of the highway create a gateway, highlighting passage between Amsterdam and Schiphol, but also giving Nieuwe Meer iconic value as a place with its own unique identity.

T4

Meandering bars of housing follow the west side of the new canal, weaving a fabric that refers back to the old geometry of farm plots and waterways. Single-loaded housing units provide light and airy living spaces with courtyards between for children to play.

12 T5

13 T6

T5

Big box retail is incorporated next to the highway. On and off ramps and parking are integrated into the building to provide efficient use of space, and decrease its footprint on the landscape.

T6

A second public interface engages the canal and its pedestrian-friendly streets. This edge is soft and welcoming, and human-scaled. Amenities enhance life for the entire district. A pier extending along the canal connects previously existing neighborhoods to the lakefront. A public plaza beneath the dike hosts a train and bus station.

14 T7

15 T8

T7

A new daycare and school is nestled between the new housing, new commercial uses, and existing playing fields.

T8

The expansion of further housing and recreation areas north of the highway links to a new elementary school. The union of retail, amenities, recreation, housing, and transit in this location make Nieuwe Meer a successful node as well as a popular destination.

Conclusion

A new kind of identity is the outcome of this transformation, one that is based on new building and infrastructure typologies rooted in local traditions. Idiosyncrasies that make the polder landscape unique are engaged in plan and section, and especially by the construction of the elevated canal. Infrastructure and buildings are neatly tied together and honor the human scale. The resulting fabric is legible and discrete in the best of Dutch planning traditions.

16 View of new highway and train overpass with a raised canal

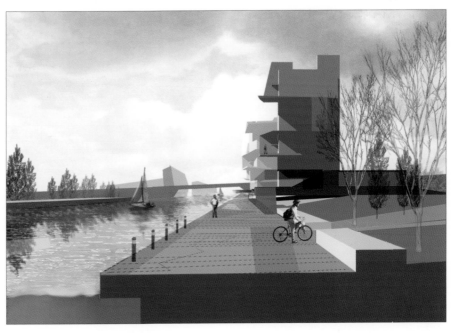

17 Housing and public space along the canal

e-Mall, Dedham, Massachusetts[1]

History

Originally settled in 1646, the town of Dedham, Massachusetts (population 23,000) sits along the banks of the Charles River on former forest and wetlands. It was home to Boston's elite until the 1900s but has evolved over time into a middle-class suburb. The road linking Boston and Providence, which later became Route 1 and links the entire eastern seaboard, passes through Dedham, and in the 1800s a railroad line was constructed parallel to Route 1. Traces of the railroad are still visible where the railroad bed has discolored the surface of the parking lot of the Dedham Mall.

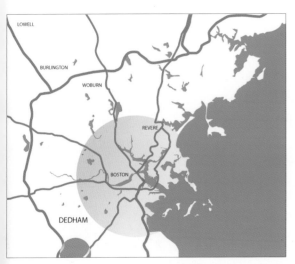

1 Locus map: Dedham

Dedham's growth was propelled by the development of major infrastructure along and through its borders, most recently Route 1 and Route 128. It has attracted significant retail development resulting in a continuous three-mile stretch of strip malls and related buildings. These retail developments are now facing competition from larger and more attractive developments in neighboring communities (Natick and Braintree).

The Dedham Mall was built in 1965 on a wedge-shaped site between Route 1 and Washington Street, a mile from Boston's Route 128 beltway to the south. It still follows the 100 percent retail two-anchor-store-surrounded-by-parking model that was developed when the mall first opened. Dedham Mall, once an attractive retail magnet, has fallen into disrepair. The prominence of this landmark has been compromised by a collection of poorly planned strip developments cluttering the edge of Route 1. The owners, intent on reconfiguring the mall, but limited by preexisting leases and agreements deliberately allowed it to fall into disrepair in order to drive out current tenants.[2] Consequently, Dedham Mall has become the favored destination of delinquent students and the elderly, who are escaping boredom.

Merely erasing the moribund mall will only produce another layer of temporally shallow development. Transforming the program to match changing economic conditions is what is really needed. The mall, the classic retail environment of the baby boomer generation, is the offspring of an automobile based economy, which requires rejuvenation. Evolving Dedham's identity as a retail center, as well as reestablishing the lost forest and wetlands and creating community links, represents the best hope for repairing this place.

Analysis: Mapping

The Charles River, as it winds through Dedham on its way to Boston Harbor, is entirely separate from Dedham's commercial strip and residential neighborhoods. Development is its own world set apart from the river, which has been squeezed into a narrow corridor of green space. A once rich network of wetlands that drains into the river has been consolidated by engineers into a rigidly defined system of culverts only legible on the landscape through a small stand of trees to the north of the mall.

2 Hydrology and greenspace

Once a dominant feature of Dedham's topography, the river has been superceded by the highway and its associated development pattern of broad throughways bisecting the community and its network of walking paths and open spaces. Bus routes follow traffic patterns and meander through parking lots, providing poor, roundabout connectivity between the mall and adjacent communities.

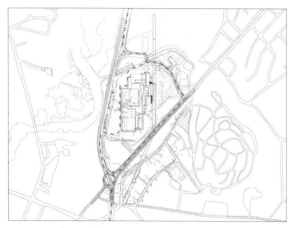

3 Traffic, bus, and pedestrian routes

Connectivity in this community is fractured and incomplete as a result, ironically, of poorly planned road and parking systems that were originally conceived of as links. These paved areas are barriers that separate one use from another, residents from workers, and children from the landscape. New linkages are needed to restore the fabric of the community and, as a by-product, enhance commercial opportunities.

The automobile-saturated environment, with its noise, pollution, and runoff, has seriously damaged environmental quality in Dedham and contributes to damage downstream. For example, oil-contaminated runoff delivers pollutants to surface and ground waters. Additionally, impermeable surfaces deliver torrents directly into waterways via the path of least resistance, contributing both to flooding and drought.

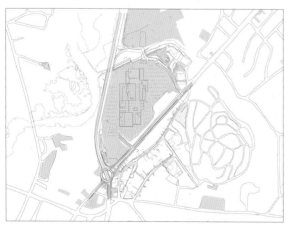

4 Paved areas

Analysis: Cross-Maps

Dedham's physical form is the result of several waves of development, each with its own set of features and geometries. The historic village southwest of the mall has its own grid that is completely segregated from the amorphous configuration of retail development along Route 1. A discrete and separate neighborhood of 1920s-era cottages, duplexes, and triple-decker housing lies to the east of the mall. The distinct qualities of each neighborhood, their building types, and road configurations are clearly legible in the figure-ground. Connectivity between these neighborhoods is damaged due to the callous layout of infrastructure, intended more for those passing through Dedham rather than the people who live there.

5 Layering history

Single-use zoning, endemic to suburbia, largely characterizes Dedham's urban fabric. Retail outlets, offices, and housing exist in isolation to one another, and are accessible only by car. This increases traffic flow, especially during high-use times (rush hour and lunchtime). Residents, workers, and shoppers alike would benefit from new building typologies that integrate or encourage linkages between uses and neighborhoods. In addition, new typologies with vibrant mixes of programs could engage the large volume of traffic on Route 1 effectively.

Parking + Landscape

While landscape features played an important role in Dedham's development, green infrastructure has been replaced by gray and environmental conditions have suffered. The highway and parking lots, with their noise, runoff, and air pollution—not to mention a microclimate that is hot in summer and blustery in winter—occupy what is a lost landscape. This asphalt savanna, however, presents an easy opportunity for restoring the lost landscape and uncovering the past, such as the train tracks and the stream system.

6 Parking + Greenspace

Design

Restoring the lost landscape, creating pedestrian connections, and incorporating new programs and typologies are key to enhancing this area's unique identity. The mall site, with its strategic location along the river and the highway, expanses of gray, monotonous parking lots, and decaying retail outlets represents the most likely area for transformation. Rather than erasing the dead mall completely, let it provide the backbone for new development and it will begin to tell a story about this place.

Opportunities Arising from Changing Retail Models

E-commerce has eroded the sales of traditional retail outlets like Dedham Mall. Online businesses minimize the number of entities separating the manufacturer from the consumer. Amazon is but one of the companies that has been successful in the new "frictionless" economy. Yet the existing model would benefit from a physical and visible presence in the marketplace. E-tail outlets (think Ikea meets barnesandnoble.com) consisting of well-located showrooms and distribution centers could combine the best features of traditional retail with the advantages of online retailing. New retail models, like e-Mall, can help revive dead malls and their communities.

T1

The existing mall is converted into a warehouse and distribution center for e-tailers. A long thin space is carved out of the front of the mall to provide a pick-up area. A sixty-foot-wide showroom is built alongside Route 1 to display e-tailers' wares to vehicular traffic along the western edge and a new pedestrian route along the eastern edge. A service zone for the warehouse occurs within the "trace" of the old rail line. An e-mall is created.

7 T1

T2

The e-mall expands southward using the same prototypical section. Additional parking needs are met with the construction of an above-grade parking structure to the rear of the service area. A new pedestrian bridge that passes through the e-mall connects Route 1 to existing housing to the east.

8 T2

T3

An artificial landscape is constructed over the existing warehouse, with new columns between existing structures to support the continuous surface of the landscape. The artificial landscape absorbs rainwater, unifies Dedham's eastern reaches with the Charles River Basin and the mall, and acts as an armature for future development above it. The trace of the old mall's circulation spine cuts through the artificial landscape, allowing light to flood into the warehouses and offices below. The first live-work spine is built alongside the pedestrian bridge spanning Route 1.

9 T3

T4

Housing and work environments are built on and over the artificial landscape. They are interspersed with open spaces and amenities such as day care, which get residents out of their cars and increase pedestrian opportunities.

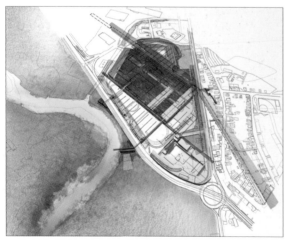

10 T4

T5

New housing and work environments bridge over a series of interconnected courtyards toward the bar of showrooms. Additional amenities such as restaurants and service-oriented shops are added alongside the circulation spines, enlivening the community experience and drawing visitors.

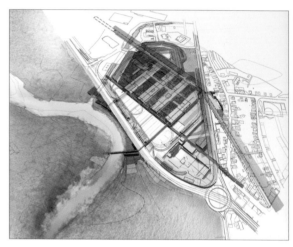

11 T5

T6

A multipurpose public space featuring playing fields and performance spaces is developed on the southwest corner of the site. Additional bridges span Route 1 and connect the e-mall community to recreational facilities along the river's edge.

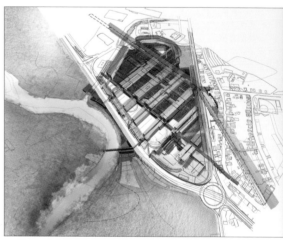

12 T6

T7

Structures of varying size and use, are built parallel to traces of the old rail line, creating a richly woven urban fabric. These developments are the second wave of structures that reconnect residential areas to the east with the e-mall site.

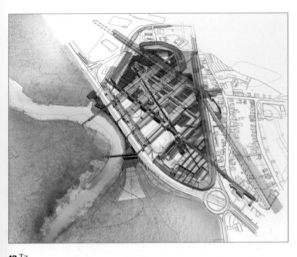

13 T7

T8

Modestly scaled towers mark important intersections and denote active places, such as the partially covered sports plaza. Housing developments continue on the northeast corner of the site, while further cuts and intensifications are made along the mall's old spine.

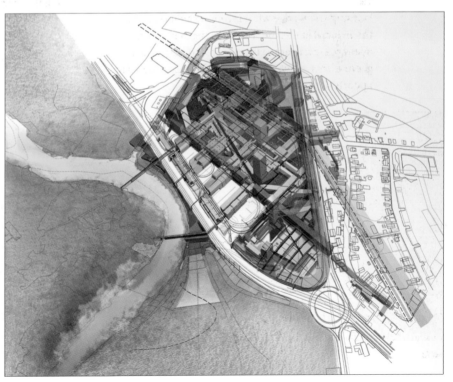

14 T8

Conclusion

A dead mall is reinvigorated with a transformation of program that tracks economic changes. Rethinking program and building typologies has the power to generate identity in communities with dying malls.

15 Cut-away perspective view of the e-mall along Route 1

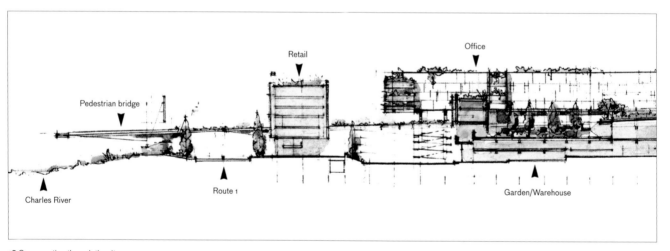

16 Cross-section through the site

Endnotes

1   This proposal for e-Mall was a finalist in the International Dead Mall Competition.

2   Since the conception of this transformation, the owners of Dedham Mall have succeeded in driving out their tenants and have reconfigured the mall as a so-called "power mall," where walking is eliminated and shoppers simply park their cars in front of the stores they wish to visit.

Shenzhen, China

History

The Louhu Customs House district in Shenzhen marks an important territorial and historic threshold that continues to evolve and change as China's social, political and economic structures transform. Twenty-five years ago, Shenzhen, was a collection of small farming and fishing villages thirty-five kilometers north of downtown Hong Kong. Today, it is a hyper-dense settlement with over ten million people built around a collection of nodes. Shenzhen is the result of Deng Xiaoping's economic reforms initiated in 1979 with the creation of new "Special Economic Zones" separated by twenty-foot iron fences. As an economic experiment where free-market policies could be practiced without harming the stability of the communist government, Shenzhen has been viewed as an unprecedented success. From a human habitat perspective, however, Shenzhen shares many of the failings of edge cities and suburbs.

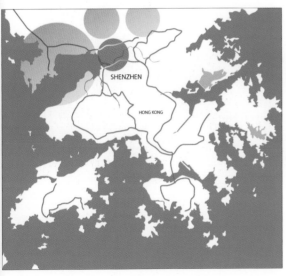

1 Locus map: Shenzhen

The Louhu Customs district is a major node in Shenzhen that exemplifies characteristics of hyper-growth similar to edge cities and suburbs—but at a scale that is unique to China and other parts of Asia. The customs house is strategically located at the southernmost tip of the bend in the Shenzhen River, which separates it from Hong Kong. The Hong Kong side of the river, with its bucolic hillsides, provides a welcome reprieve to the high-density development of the Shenzhen side. This border crossing is extremely busy for pedestrians and train passengers, but not for cars. Over a million people pass through the gates during the Chinese New Year, for example. A new train station was built just north of the customs house after 1979 to accommodate cross-border transit, but the train systems are not yet connected. Passengers traveling between Shenzhen and Hong Kong must disembark, cross the river, and re-embark on a new train to complete their journey.

Since 1979, this district has evolved into a full-fledged downtown of sorts, with residential, commercial, and hotel towers clustered in close proximity to the train station. Retail centers, bus stops, subway stations, smaller scale housing, fish ponds, random patches of landscape, and even old military bunkers are interwoven by a system of roads, ramps, tunnels, and bridges.

Analysis: Mapping

A figure-ground drawing reveals a collection of building types of different scales and configurations organized in somewhat fragmentary swatches, reflecting an ad-hoc development process. Patches of small-scale housing to the northeast of the station predate the mega development period and constitute a vernacular neighborhood of sorts. In contrast, the size of the train station, and the mall (to its southeast), and hotel complex (to its northeast), illustrate the radical scale shifts so commonly found in emerging economies. Together, these three structures create the beginnings of a town square, whose fourth side (to the east) is poorly defined, creating a diffuse spatial edge.

2 A Chinese edge city in Shenzhen, China

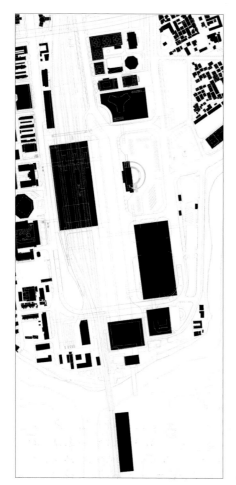

3 Figure-ground

where they can board trains. Secondary streams of pedestrian traffic run perpendicular and diagonally across the transit plaza. The heavily trafficked routes provide few easy connections to the riverside.

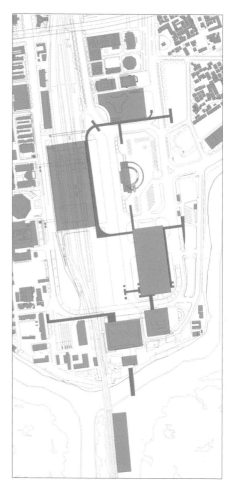

4 Elevated traffic

The customs house sits across from the Hong Kong train station to its south and across the river. Its prominent position is strategically located, offering uninterrupted vistas north and south. The remaining building fabric is a mix of building types, towers, town houses, and miscellaneous structures of various sizes and shapes, filling in voids where land is available.

The primary stream of movement runs along the north-south axis linking Shenzhen to Hong Kong. Pedestrian traffic is especially heavy just north of the train station, as travelers board and disembark from trains and head across the great expanses of asphalt fields toward the customs house. This terrain is contested, by the presence of buses and taxis. Once travelers have been processed through the customs house, they traverse the pedestrian bridge, toward the Hong Kong station,

Little shade is offered to commuters as they make their way on foot from one train system to the other. The shadow patterns taken mid-morning on a summer day, show the lack of shade, especially around the pedestrian paths to and from the train station and the customs house. Conversely, towers to the north create dense canyon-like spaces with little access to the direct sunlight, which is a very important factor in Chinese residential design.

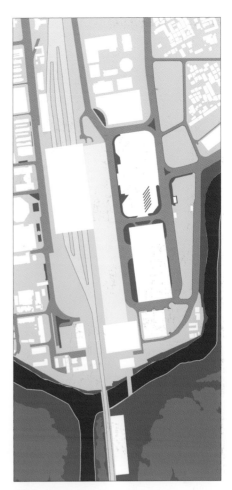

6 Gray + Green spaces

5 Shadows

Analysis: Cross-Mapping

Paved, impervious surfaces dominate the Shenzhen landscape, while the natural landscape is largely preserved on the Hong Kong side of the river. Small parcels of landscape are sprinkled around Shenzhen without a discernable plan, nor are they connected in a way that creates a network of green spaces. Cross-mapping gray versus green space demonstrates the need to create a series of interconnected green spaces.

A large figural public area in front of the train station is defined by a fringe of trees, where travelers enjoy a welcome reprieve from the sun. Many of the remaining green spaces in Shenzhen have no trees, or shade, making it uninviting or unbearable to be outdoors in this city 22 degrees above the equator. The Hong Kong side of the river is well shaded by trees, which helps reduce ambient temperatures, and provides cues for transforming Shenzhen.

What does provide some shade are the ramps, elevated roads, bridges, and rail lines that make up the dense network of infrastructure integrated with complimentary systems, existing buildings, and streets. The geometry required of each system generates unusual configurations though. The radius of an elevated ramp, for example, does not always create satisfactory or inhabitable ground level spaces as it negotiates around pre-existing structures. Still, the ramp patterns are distinctive, and prominent in the Customs House district. They could provide welcome shade below their spans if the spaces underneath were programmed and designed for pedestrian uses.

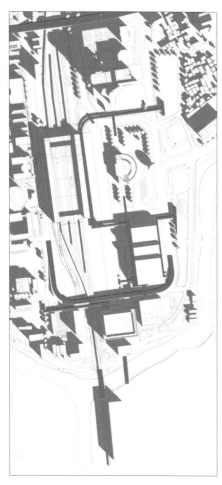

7 Ramps + Shadows

Design

This environment is inhospitable to the millions of visitors that traverse its great expanses of asphalt without relief from the tropical sunshine. It also lacks the kind of public open spaces that make up great international cities. However, as the economic and political role of this border crossing evolves, urban form can evolve as well. There is also an opportunity to record the current form and uses of this site before they are swept away by increasing integration between Hong Kong and China.

T1

Voids in the urban fabric, so clearly illustrated in the figure-ground drawing, are sites which can be developed as new multi-use structures (housing and ground floor retail). This first phase of infill helps to better define the main public space as a public square.

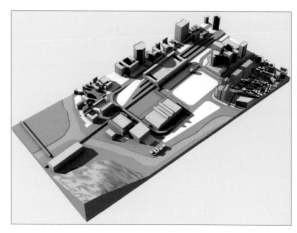

8 T1

T2

The north-south pedestrian route connecting the Shenzhen train station to the customs house could be etched into the landscape to a three-meter depth to record the historical movement of people across borders. Pedestrians will enjoy shade from morning and afternoon sun created by the walls of the walkway, and will be protected from overhead rays by a canopy of trees. This new promenade acts as an armature that connects the train station to public space to the east.

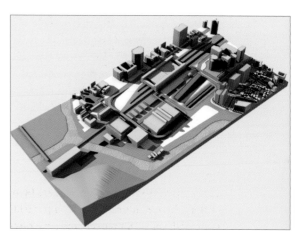

9 T2

T3

The existing mall is ripe for expansion given the volume of pedestrian traffic. The structure's architectural quality can be redefined and strengthened to relate to the newly defined promenade and public square using transformations of wrapping, enveloping, and morphing.

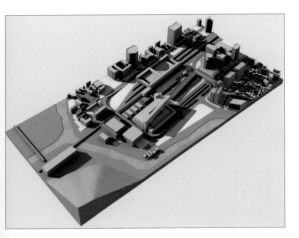

10 T3

T4

The spatial definition of the public plaza is completed with the infill of the parcels located between the plaza and square. These buildings also help in defining the river's edge, a vastly underutilized amenity and resource.

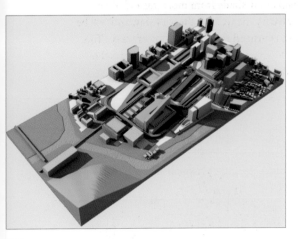

11 T4

T5

Further riverfront development takes hold west of the customs house, in a scale that compliments the size and grain of the adjacent parcels and structures.

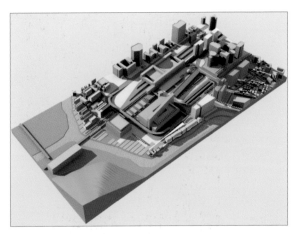

12 T5

T6

As the political and economic necessity for a border crossing disappears over time, the customs house itself is transformed into a ruin of sorts, to be reinhabited as a destination in itself. New parks and paths circumscribe the perimeter of the traces of this void, commemorating the memory of a nation divided, but now connected. Increased traffic between points north and south can be further accommodated by the addition of small-scale bridges, and a new tunnel excavated beneath the Shenzhen River.

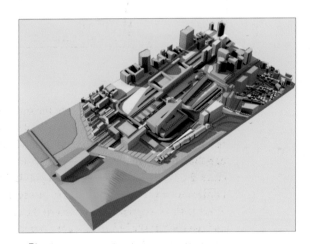

13 T6

T7

The last remaining parcels, in and around the rail station lines, bridges, and ramps are infilled with new structures whose swooping forms follow the geometry of the adjacent infrastructure.

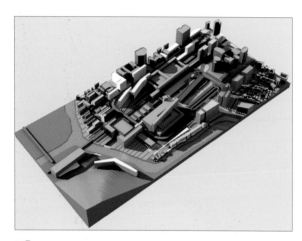

14 T7

Conclusion

This transformation is meant to improve the experience of a mega-edge city for its millions of visitors and inhabitants. Rapid development created less than desirable spaces and places; but they can be repaired over time, and new identities can emerge. The design process anticipates changing territorial conditions that will make the customs house obsolete, and marks this area for a rebirth. The border area cannot only create better connectivity between Hong Kong and Shenzhen, but can itself become a destination with a unique identity shaped by the qualities of the site, and changing economic and political circumstances. Buildings, and public spaces are transformed to create a more sustainable and enticing environment, which can help heal the schisms of the past.

T8

Publicly accessible green spaces along the river mirror the preserve on the Hong Kong side, and improve quality of life for residents and provide a cohesive experience for cross-border visitors.

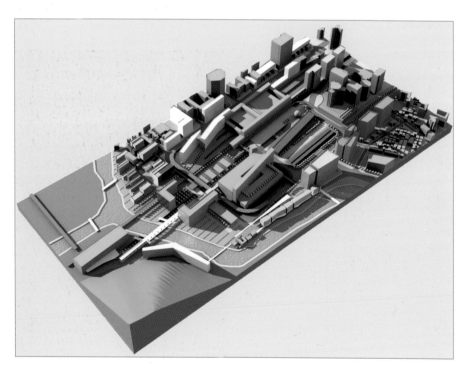

15 T8

16 Daytime view of plaza in front of train station, looking south toward customs house and Hong Kong

17 Nighttime view

18 View of new riverscape integrated into the landscape

19 Aerial view looking south toward Hong Kong

Revere Beach, Massachusetts

History

Five miles north of Boston is a well-known coastal landmark, Revere Beach. The first naval battle of the revolutionary war took place off this beach in 1775. To Bostonians, it conjures images of a "North Shore" beach community and its varied inland landscape characterized by sand, salt marshes, gently rolling drumlins, and grasslands. The land, rich in fish and game, was originally inhabited by the Pawtucket Indians. European settlers arrived in Rumney Marsh, as it was known in the 1630s. Subsequently, Rumney Marsh was parceled into twenty-one lots that were later consolidated into seven large farms. Rumney Marsh was annexed to Boston in 1634, and Chelsea in 1739. In 1914 the city of Revere was incorporated, the city's name paying tribute to that famous revolutionary and alluding to its colonial history.

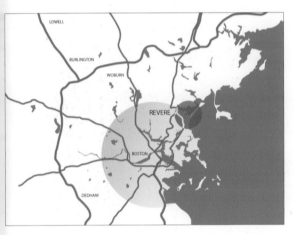

1 Locus map: Revere Beach

Revere prospered as a farming community well into the 1800s, but real change was brought on by the development of rail lines servicing Revere and points north. In 1838 the first rail line was constructed by Eastern Railroad. And in 1875 the Revere Beach & Lynn Railroad, was constructed on a berm of sand separating the beach from the boulevard. Revere Beach suddenly became a preferred summer weekend destination for Bostonians seeking a respite from the city. Revere's popularity exploded and spurred rapid, often haphazard, development along its beach front, primarily related to recreation and entertainment.

In 1896, The Metropolitan Parks Commission acquired all the land abutting the beach and created the beach reservation which required setting the rail line back one hundred yards inland. Charles Eliot, a renowned Harvard-trained landscape architect, developed the master plan for the beach reservation. His plan, whose traces are still evident today, called for a double boulevard plan with strategically located public spaces, buildings, and pavilions.

Revere's golden era extended until the 1940s during which time the beach witnessed the construction of major attractions, such as the Wonderland Park, an amusement park (1905), The Cyclone roller coaster (1927), and Wonderland Greyhound Park and Suffolk Downs Racing Track (1935). By the beginning of World War II, Revere's population had spiked to 34,405. Its population continued to grow to over 40,000 in the 1950s as Boston Subway (the Blue Line) was extended to Revere. A commuter line linking Boston to northern suburbs cut through Revere, one-quarter-mile west of the beach.

The Beach, however, did begin its steady decline as a desirable recreational destination in the 1950s as options of mobility and recreational outlets increased. Consequently significant landmarks were torn down: the Bath House in 1962 and roller coaster in 1972. The final blow came in 1978, when a massive blizzard destroyed many businesses along the boulevard.

Since then, attempts have been made to revitalize the beachfront and surrounding districts, achieving mixed results. Terraced concrete towers were built along the Beach's southern flank, and pavilions and some historic beachfront structures have been restored. To the west of the site, large parking lots border the dog run and strip developments along Route 1A, a major artery connecting Boston to northern suburbs. Today, new plans to capitalize on Revere's unique location are under development. As a place on the edge (the edge of the city, edge of the landscape) and connected by multiple rail systems and major arteries to points beyond, its development potential is extremely valuable.

Analysis: Mapping

As an intermodal transit hub, Revere is uniquely positioned as a nexus for local and regional residents. The commuter rail line that borders the Wonderland racetrack is well suited to provide connections to the residents and visitors alike. However, it is separated from the Blue Line subway by barriers such as a parking lot and busy Route 1A, which make crossing between the two train lines inconvenient, unpleasant, and even dangerous. Stronger pedestrian connections here could increase ridership and commuter activity, by making it an easy crossroads and gateway for people passing between Boston and outlying North Shore communities.

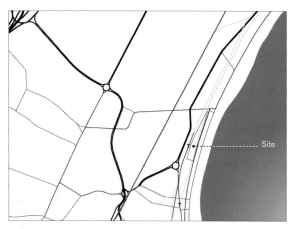

2 Infrastructure: subway, railway, highway, and avenues

Rail stations offer a unique opportunity for what is known as transit-oriented development—development positioned along transit lines that can minimize automobile usage. Offices, retail amenities, and residences located within a quarter of a mile of a rail station will attract commuters, shoppers, and residents who can largely abandon their cars in favor of the ease and convenience of mass transit. Parking needs are reduced and higher value uses can be programmed in these areas. With its two subway stations, Revere Beach has a large area that is suitable for transit-oriented development, but it is currently dominated by land-use patterns and infrastructure that excludes the pedestrian.

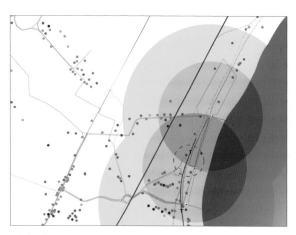

3 Pedestrian access: 200-yard radius from subway stops

Concentrations of restaurants, stores, churches, schools, entertainment establishments, and government services currently lie along well-traveled automobile routes, but along the transit corridor, there is a large "black hole" dominated by parking lots. This area could be developed to serve a much higher density and variety of uses, given improved pedestrian and automobile access. Thousands of drivers each day speed by Revere Beach to run errands, shop, and amuse themselves elsewhere.

4 Programs: coffee shops, retail, schools, and churches

Site Ecology

The original Rumney Marsh, once rich in fish and game, has been grossly violated over the last fifty years in particular. The protected sand barriers, the beach, the fresh and salt water marshes, canals, and ponds are all part of larger ecosystems. The landscape and the wildlife it supports are an important part of the identity of this community, sandwiched between sea and terra firma. Wetlands are now protected by federal law, but components of the salt and freshwater systems in Revere have already been built upon, paved, or culverted.

5 Sensitive ecologies: wetlands to the north

Community Fabric

The figure-ground map clearly shows how Revere's neighborhoods have evolved over time. Discrete street and block patterns are oriented to accommodate primary roadways, topography or adjacent neighborhoods. These maps also show that the continuity of this fabric has been damaged or severed through erasure brought about by the large-scale development of the dog run and adjacent strip mall development, as well as the transit stations. How can the integrity of Revere's morphology be regenerated?

6 Figure-ground + Parks

Analysis: Cross-Mapping

Superimposing Revere's infrastructure and ecological features shows how the natural routes for waterways have been severed (by rail lines or major roadways) or rerouted along tortuous paths via concrete culverts, so as to avoid parking lots and large buildings. Is there a way to reconsider the spatial distribution of waterways, rail lines, and roadways in a more reciprocal manner, so that each can coexist, even as a kind of new infrastructure?

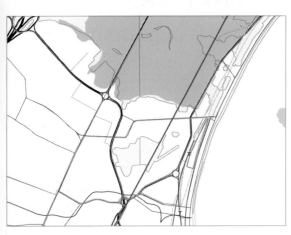

7 Infrastructure + Ecology

It is not only the buildings that contribute to creating a cohesive sense of community. The distribution and location of uses (especially the publicly oriented uses) ideally should be coordinated with the shapes and networks of pubic spaces and the buildings that define them. While Revere has many patches of strong building fabric, with continuous and well-organized commercial and institutional programs, many large voids break up Revere's overall community structure. The great "black hole" left in the community's fabric by parking lots creates a spatial and programmatic chasm difficult to span for programs and single buildings. A fabric or buildings, uses and landscape are required to fill this void and connect neighborhoods.

8 Figure-ground + Zoning

Design

Any transformation of Revere should be sensitive to the landscape and its ecosystems, and honor its unique historic and current role as a place between places, where multiple transportation systems intersect, yet are poorly connected.

The lack of connections between different systems results in part from the destruction of urban fabric and mix of uses that are so important in knitting communities together. Thus commuters rarely stop here, or engage the community, because it is a poorly defined place between places, lacking a strong identity.

Building on the strengths of Revere's history, its landscape, and infrastructure system are the keys to reviving this community. Integrated infrastructure systems and links to walkable public landscape will improve its function and identity as a gateway, destination, and crossroads. Strengthening and repairing the morphology of the working class neighborhoods adjacent to the beachfront, by filling in and extending street and block patterns, will include the larger community rather than shut them out.

T1

A well designed intermodal station supporting subway, bus lines, and parking helps to anchor future developments. The bus and rail stations are beneath a raised green plaza (an artificial landscape) and are bounded by new structures on four sides, creating a strongly defined public space. The rotary on Route 1A is reconfigured as a triangular space, more in keeping with geometry of existing Revere neighborhoods.

9 T1

T2

Creating a prominent presence on the waterfront is achieved through the dramatic design of towers (with commercial and cultural uses) sandwiched between the new intermodal station and Revere Beach Boulevard. In addition, a conservatory occupies the triangular plaza, allowing for year around activities. The crystalline geometry of the towers and conservatory respond in part to the intersecting sight lines generated by Route 1A from the north and the VFW Parkway from the southwest, both providing major physical and visual access to the beach, something that is currently lacking.

10 T2

T3

A new neighborhood fabric is created along Ocean Avenue, by extending the street pattern of adjacent neighborhoods into this development area. Comprised primarily of housing and small-scale commercial and recreational uses, this new neighborhood creates a strong edge along the beachfront. Each block's courtyard is connected to a new landscape armature, which runs north to south and connects to the intermodal station. This landscape builds off the existing wetlands and tidal pools and sensitive ecology.

11 T3

T4

The new landscape armature extends in a southern direction and services the existing towers facing the beach (to the east) and a new strip of commercial and office related uses to the west. New courtyards would feed into the landscape armature, as well as provide connections to the beach, where walls once divided neighborhoods and districts.

12 T4

T5

Connections between the beach and neighborhoods across from Route 1A—a major barrier—are created by extending Atwood Street from its origins at St. Anthony's Parish eastward, over the commuter rail line, across Route 1A and toward the beach, where it is transformed into a pier that reaches deep into the bay. The pier recalls the ferries that used to service the beach in the nineteenth century, but also creates an important public space linked by pedestrian access deep into Revere.

13 T5

T6

The large parking fields at Wonderland Park are finally converted into new multi-use developments with naturally landscaped gardens tied to the native ecology.

Major commercial and retail uses bound Route 1A, capitalizing on heavy vehicular traffic and prominent visibility. The Wonderland Park (dog run) is converted into new recreational fields and stadiums. A new station is built for the commuter rail, and offers shuttle services to the intermodal station, linking previously disconnected services.

14 T6

T7

The large strip mall to the south of Wonderland Park, and its vacuous parking lots, are converted into a more vibrant district with improved land-use efficiencies. The parking lot is filled with low (twenty-foot-high) green terraced structures housing parking and warehouses. A housing bar is built over the existing mall, and is cut through its footprint to create a new street, tying new developments with the fabric of adjacent neighborhoods. A larger elevated commercial structure defines the edges along the VFW and the North Shore Road.

15 T7

T8

The last frame illustrates the incremental infill of sites on the former Wonderland parkway site, as courtyards gradually are filled in with smaller structures. Similarly, new structures and uses reinhabit the existing concrete terraced towers.

16 T8

Conclusion

This scenario study demonstrates how a badly scarred landscape, lacking discernable qualities of place, can be transformed over time to create a place where the reconstituted presence of the landscape is complemented by higher value uses. The result is a new fabric of neighborhoods, reflecting Revere's rich history, yet serving as a nexus of activities and infrastructure.

17 View from the Atlantic

18 Site plan integrating natural systems, infrastructure, historic neighborhoods, and new uses and typologies.

19 View toward the Atlantic from the east

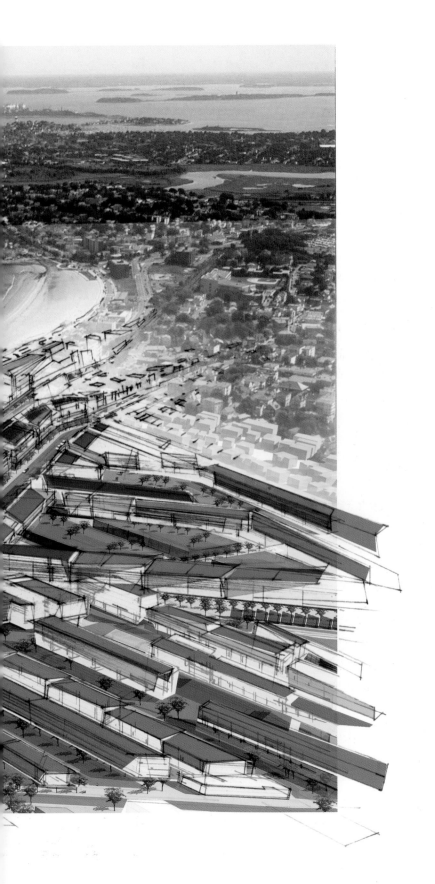

Significance of the Proposition

This book began by questioning whether or not we can create environments and communities that we are proud of, in the values they represent, and in the form and spaces they have taken on. Presented rhetorically, the postulation that an edge city could evolve into Venice or its equivalent in urban beauty is a stretch—or is it? Can we begin to transform the banal into the sublime, and in the process remedy the pathologies of present day suburbia: mismanaged resources, disappearing community life, poor environmental quality, and lack of identity?

The proposition put forth in this book is not presented as a panacea; instead, it offers a new way of reading the clues and traces of our present environments. There is no guaranteed remedy for all of suburbia, for such a remedy can only result from the will exercised by those that have the interest and the power to effect such a change. Adequate resources, power, and good fortune are required to transform our edge cities over time into better and more habitable places. In the context of the arguments set forth in this book, the significant contributions of the Adaptive Design Process are outlined below.

Suburban Palimpsests: Enriching Community Identity

The Adaptive Design Process provides a conceptual framework for transforming communities over time, so that they might evolve into places with unique identities, distinguishable from other edge cities and their suburban contexts. This framework arises from engaging a site's "useful history" and discouraging the ever-present development tendency to "erase" completely all traces of past "writings" and landscape. This proposition promotes the development of new multi-layered configurations of communities, where the richly intertwined relationships between physical, social, economic, and natural systems are brought into a dynamic yet sustaining balance. The relationship between past actions, current conditions, and future possibilities are illuminated, revealing time's transformative power. People are oriented in these new environments by physical and temporal landmarks that register an evolving fabric in a community's collective consciousness. Associations generated through the interaction of time, place, and circumstance generate integral, not applied, meaning for a community and its members. These evolving suburban palimpsests have the power to generate deeply rooted places, places anchored to the landscape and to society.

New Processes / The Adaptive Design Process

This book presents tangible and practical processes, methodologies, and tools to generate suburban "palimpsests."

They are means of linking data, design, and experience as communities seek to find the fit between their community's form and its intended use, and all its associations. This process is not meant to impede spontaneous and idiosyncratic actions, actions that break the rules or evolutionary trends. Instead, it offers a way to record, register, and remind stakeholders of the consequences and opportunities implicit in their actions. Mindful and informed decisionmaking improves the chance of building thoughtfully conceived environments. The balanced application of analytical tools can guide the creation of well-tempered environments, embrace unusual circumstances, honor the accidents of history, and enrich the identity of place.

Simulating Future Changes, Heightening Awareness of Future Possibilities

Understanding the complexity of your current environment is already difficult without imagining how the forces of time might play themselves out in the future. In addition, the complexity of these environments is so daunting in scale that it makes it difficult for the general public, and even planners, to imagine how edge city contexts could change. The Adaptive Design Process gives communities the power to represent, through simulations, how their communities might change over time. To see the wide array of alternatives is an empowering and liberating experience that can allow interested parties to activate change. The search for the proper strategies for transforming environments can be tested against performance criteria. The probability of meeting goals through tactical plans can be fine-tuned before and during design and construction, and can be recalibrated as circumstances change.

By-Products

Besides its immediate benefits, the Adaptive Design Process offers a number of other beneficial by-products.

Digital Applications

The Adaptive Design Process, when coupled with existing GIS and design software tools, can provide planners, developers, designers, and community groups with a powerful digital platform for analyzing and redesigning communities. A platform could be developed to allow for a number of plug-in applications, for analytical as well as design (typological) tools.

Documenting and Codifying Transformations

The nature and behavior of change in urban environments is difficult to understand historically and even more difficult to predict. This book offers an introduction to a code, or language, of erasure and writing, which can begin to help dissect the incremental changes brought about to buildings and their contexts, on all scales. By stringing together the operations of change (erasure and writing), the history of each object in a city, as well as the city as a whole, can be analyzed. Such models can uncover patterns of change, as more than random occurrences, and as very much tied to discernable interactions of time, place, and circumstance. An increased awareness of these processes will allow us to design environments mindful of time's arrow.

Tools and Typologies

The Adaptive Design Process has documented a number of design tools and typologies useful in transforming suburbs. They operate at both conceptual and pragmatic levels and at varying scales. We have borrowed typologies developed by others and generated new ones. The method of classification proposed and its emphasis on hybrid typologies invites new typological invention. It is the development of such typologies, and their specific applications, deeply rooted to site conditions, which will allow communities to develop unique identities.

Suburban Morphology

Anne Vernez Moudon emphasizes the need to understand suburban typologies and uses conventional morphological analytical tools to dissect suburban sites. Figure-ground analysis and other morphological analytical tools are limited. What is required is a broader inclusion of tools for analyzing the morphology of suburbs. The case studies in this book begin to indicate a richness of analysis generated through the study of suburban morphology and its need on a more extensive scale. In addition, the book provides a wide array of tools for analyzing the suburban morphology. We are generating new communities outside our city centers at an extraordinary pace, yet we do not have all the analytical tools we need to understand the fabric that has evolved, or the ability to develop more convincing alternatives that might arise out of such an analysis.

Issues and Problems

This book is about urban design. The five cases depict visionary transformations; that is, they are developed with an eye toward promoting idealized spatial and formal conditions. Form, space, landscape, and infrastructure are configured to create powerful and memorable spaces, dynamic yet rooted to their sites. All of the images illustrated in the book are buildable, and many of the buildings shown use standard construction systems. But in the real world, other factors like ownership, parceling, zoning, infrastructure, density, traffic, parking, public and private cooperation, who is in control, finance, and marketability contribute to the development and construction of suburban communities. Such factors are considered in this book, but they did not drive ultimate form in each case study. Time allows for the inclusion of these factors, though, which are often design determinants. Their integration can make for a richer and more complex place, truly reflecting the circumstances, forces, and players that exercise influence, control, and power over what is built over time.

Ownership

Who owns the property, who controls it, and who inhabits it? What rights do they have in determining its future? The American legal system has long recognized the sanctity of property rights. These rights are often in direct conflict with community interests. What mechanisms can be exercised to encourage property owners to build with the broader interests of the community in mind?

Parceling

Unlike traditional cities, which often evolve from regularized grids laid out by surveyors, the suburban landscape's parceling is more complicated. Parceling may result from variations in the topography, the division of farms, or the complex history of sales and trades between landowners. Even more complex are the corporate reconfigurations of plots to correspond to leasing and contractual agreements between owners and leasers.

How does the community, its leaders, and designers, reconcile the often-convoluted parcel configurations with more desirable and optimal design options? This question is especially challenging in light of the book's premise, namely that the idiosyncratic nature of a site, revealed through its mapping, can generate a unique community.

Zoning

As has been well-documented in the writings of Andres Duany and Elizabeth Plater-Zyberk, zoning policies and practices have had a profound effect on shaping suburban communities. The CNU has developed superior alternate models to current laws, yet the time, legal effort, and community commitment required to overcome current practices can be overwhelming.

How then should communities proceed? Do they meet their long-term objectives by granting variances case by case? Or do towns and planning departments need to revamp their zoning based on strategic projections? And, if so, can the new ordinances be written with sufficient flexibility to support a recalibration of a strategic vision as circumstances dictate?

Infrastructure

Infrastructure requires a significant investment of time and resources on the part of municipal governments, states, and federal agencies. The funding mechanisms are complicated and engineering constraints are limiting. Many of the proposals made in the book challenge the limits of these regulations, yet models for implementing similar concepts have been tested and implemented in Europe and Asia. The question then arises, can designs deviating slightly from federal guidelines be approved? And how can the development and funding of infrastructure projects be coordinated with private development, especially for those "hybrid typologies" where infrastructure, land, and buildings merge?

Density

The case studies generally add higher densities to their target sites. The assumption is that the U.S. population will continue to increase, and existing communities along the edge of metropolitan areas will continue to grow. The experience of edge cities in general indicate that a reluctance to plan or endorse growth cannot delay the inevitable.

Given the fact of growth, how much development can edge cities absorb? How will the transition be made from lower density districts to compact communities? How will multi-use strategies be integrated into single-use zoning conventions? How will the lifestyles of residents be affected? And how will it change the relationship of a satellite community to other similar communities and the metropolitan area as a whole?

Traffic and Parking

Traffic engineering is a complex field, influenced by the subtlest actions of individual drivers (rubber-neckers) as well as larger global trends. As American cars have gotten bigger, their environmental and spatial impact has increased. It follows that if densities are likely to increase, that a similar adjustment in traffic capacity cannot be accommodated within the limits of the current model. Further complicating this formula is the impact that increased densities will have on parking. Parking requires space, which in most of the book's proposals was achieved by integrating parking structures under buildings and within berms, hills, artificial landscapes, and in underutilized space next to highways. All of these solutions are expensive, and can only be realized if the value of the new buildings exceed the increased costs.

How then can new models of transportation be integrated into the development of these communities? What alternatives to the single car, single occupant model are viable and attractive (the Zip car)? How can public transportation, time-shared parking lots, and other science fiction-inspired technical innovations (Segways and moving sidewalks) free up our reliance on the car? How much of an impact can we realistically assume that higher densities, mixed uses, improved proximity to work, and other concepts put forth in this book will have on improving our current models of transportation?

Public and Private Coordination

Some parts of the proposed visions will require public sector participation, especially those involving infrastructure. How will the long-term interests of funders be protected? How will the development aims of private developers be coordinated with public interests to match the construction, financings, and operation of infrastructure? Where public and private interests are intertwined as part of a larger development, how can roles and domains of each party be coordinated, while keeping the larger community in mind?

Who are the players? Who controls the process?

By definition, the Adaptive Design Process engages any and all stakeholders in a community. The process can be used to create a more transparent and level playing field for all parties with an interest in how their communities develop. Community advocates can use it to reveal to developers the long-term consequences of their proposals, allowing for refinements and alternatives to be tested. Similarly, developers can use this process to foster community support for their initiatives. Town planners can develop an "evolving" archive of past, current, and proposed developments.

Who funds and finances this process? Is it the burden of the developer or the town? What mechanisms can be developed to allow for all parties to contribute commensurate to their respective roles, scale of projects, and available resources? Once the Adaptive Design Process is introduced, who takes the lead in monitoring and controlling the process? How is the information distributed and to which parties? Who has the right to test simulations? Who pays for the service?

Finance

Clearly, some of the designs proposed in this book challenge conventional development and finance models. Financiers are willing to finance the prevalent big-box model because the results are supposedly predictable. This predictability reduces the risk to the investors and the bank. New development models and prototypes presumably increase investment risk. However, the continued closure of hundreds of malls, strip malls, and speculative office constructions calls these assumptions into question. The development cycles of many of these developments require increasingly short financial lifecycles (as little as five years) to be considered viable.

Are there ways in which the financing mechanisms and risk assessment can take into account the advantages of projects that are deeply rooted to a community's economic needs as well as its identity? Can the design and financing of building lifecycle components be broken down and coordinated with one another, such that the term of a financing mechanism is more strongly linked to the physical lifecycle of building components? (This already happens to some degree in the financing of tenant fit out spaces—office or retail.)

Marketability: You will build it, but will they come?

It can be argued that the current models of development have evolved through a careful calibration of what the "market" wants and what it will pay. But are strip malls and big boxes really what the market demands? Does the public want to see its landscape desecrated? Or are these models of development dominant because public and developers are not fully aware of other options? Is it a question of greed: Do rock bottom prices and maximized profits really outweigh a healthy environment and real quality of life?

Looking at the incremental transformation of a site, different and innovative concepts can be tested *in situ*. The Adaptive Design Process therefore allows for new marketing and financial models to be tested as prototypes, in order to evaluate their viability before they are actually built. Furthermore, because the Adaptive Design Process is designed to reflect the community's mandate, it is more likely that the community, further enhancing its prospects for marketing and economic success, will welcome new projects.

Next Steps: This Is for You

This book began with the question of whether or not we can transform current communities into more sustainable and habitable environments. Can we convert the banality of so many of our edge cities into memorable environments, ones that people will seek out to live in, work in, and visit? This book has focused on the design attributes, tools, and processes that might bring about the transformation of suburban communities. Multiple scenarios and visions have been presented to illustrate just some of the positive outcomes that can result from this process. The possibilities, especially when considering the options for phasing, are infinite. There are no limits to how time and circumstance can come together to create new communities that are deeply rooted to place.

What then are the next steps? How will this massive undertaking, the transformation of suburban communities, be realized? Who will initiate this process? Who will run it? Who will control it? What are the respective roles of all the players in the process? What can each of us do to bring about this future?

This book, and the process it sets forth, is an invitation to all parties who currently have an interest and a stake in a community to participate in its transformation, directly or through representation. The book is about creating an "open" field, where information and design can flow freely, backwards and forwards in time, so that the interaction of forces operating on this field can be engaged, recombined, and tested to determine the probability of generating a good fit between proposed designs and current and future needs.

Sometimes, the biggest obstacle in transforming our circumstances is our inability to envision the future. This book arms those who have the desire to see their communities change with images of what the transformation of their physical environment might look like, and how it might be realized over time. As such it is a powerful tool, one that can be employed on all scales, large and small. This tool can be built from the top down or bottom up, or both simultaneously. Listed below are just a few examples of whom this process might benefit.

→ Individual corporate, retail, and office owners can use this process to plan the operation, maintenance, and renovation of their properties over the term of their projected ownership. Projects can range from large office or mall complexes to individual buildings. Owners of adjacent properties can tether their virtual models incrementally to create a simulation of their evolving community.

→ Developers proposing new projects can use this tool to convince communities that their proposed designs are likely to yield positive results in the short and long term.

→ Institutions (hospitals, colleges, churches, etc.) can project their needs to enlarge their facilities, and test the viability of expansion plans that might impact neighboring communities.

→ Federal, state, and local governments can test proposals for infrastructure projects, not only in terms of their impact on the physical environment, but also their perceptual impact (especially sight and sound).

→ Local governments can create databases that are built up incrementally over time to represent a community's current condition and how it can be transformed over time. This process allows for individual proposals to be "plugged" in and tested against community backed design standards.

→ Environmental groups, affordable housing advocates, and other community oriented groups can use this process to promote and protect public interests by communicating the negative impact of certain proposals, as well as alternatives.

This book is an invitation for all those interested in changing their environments to exercise their imaginations and their rights. The power rests with you, and those you encourage to support and endorse a shared vision for the future. Time is our ally when we are conscious of its power to transform.

Index